C000142625

ROAD TO ROMANIA

ROAD
TO ROMANIA

'Glimpses of God's Glory'
Stories to Encourage and
Inspire

By

ANN PENROSE

The proceeds from the sale of this book will be
donated to the work of Support for Romania
Registered Charity Number: 1007614

First published 2007
Reprinted 2014

Published by: Support for Romania,
26 Mavis Grove,
Rhiwbina,
Cardiff.
CF14 4SA

ISBN 978-0-9557094-0-1

Following the demand for copies of *'Road to Romania'* which resulted in no more being available, the trustees have decided to issue a reprint.

We are grateful to the Lord for the blessing that has attended the book and for the way in which lives have been changed as people have seen 'How great is our God'.

Ann Penrose

Printed by J & P Davison
3 James Place, Treforest, Pontypridd.
Mid Glamorgan. CF37 1SQ

This book is dedicated to all those dear people
who have supported this work for many years
in so many different ways. A special thanks to all
who work in both the warehouses, for doing ordinary
tasks with such love and great zeal. I hope it will give
you an insight, not only into the work,
but a realisation also that we serve an amazing
God. Thank you for enabling us to help those
who are so less fortunate than ourselves.
Together we can make a difference.

Acknowledgements

My grateful thanks to:

Ed Swires-Hennessy who first encouraged me to put my writings into print.

Janet Wing for her expertise on the computer.

Rev Roy Jenkins who further encouraged me along the road.

Brian & Rhydian Topley for their proof reading, correcting, and helping with the photographs.

My dear husband, Alan, who has helped me in ways far too numerous to mention (as he always does!)

Simon John for his excellence in interpreting my wishes for the book cover.

Lastly but most importantly, Rev Owen Milton who, from the wealth of his experience has so diligently helped me in putting this book together.

'Owen, I appreciate so much all your hard work, time and patience. I could not have done it without you.'

Commendation

I have written introductions to many books and commendations for many others, and the words always came very easily. But now, in front of this book I am sort of speechless! There are too many things that I would like to say all at once! This book is rich in wonderful and amazing stories about so many dedicated people in Great Britain who sacrificially do and give so much to help the poor people of Romania. There are many moving stories about these Romanian Christians, unbelievably poor but so faithful to the Lord in spite of their utter poverty!

The book is rich in content and it is beautifully written. It shows disarming sincerity in telling stories of personal blunders or shortcomings. But what a nobility of character is demonstrated even in this sincerity.

Ann Penrose has given us a moving story about a group of generous people who have done so much to help the people in need in Romania. Thank you Ann, both for what you and Alan and your friends have done for us in Romania, and thank you also for telling us this story in such a delightfully skilful way.

Josef Ton of Romania

Contents

Introduction

For a long time I have had a burning desire to put down on paper the wonderful ways in which we have seen the Lord work as we travel back and forth to Romania.

So, here they are. I do hope that they will encourage you to see what a wonderful God we have - how He is interested in every detail of our lives, how there is nothing that escapes His notice, and how He goes to tremendous trouble to make sure that His plans are fulfilled in an individual's life.

"For I know the plans I have for you," declares
the Lord, "plans to prosper you and not to harm
you, plans to give you hope and a future."
Jeremiah 29:11. *The Living Bible.*

Foreword

I looked at my watch; it was two o'clock in the morning and twenty degrees below freezing. We had now been here three hours waiting to enter Romania. Our papers were correct but the border guards were just being awkward. Apparently this was usual.

"What", I asked myself, "is a fifty-year-old woman doing here?"

I thought of my comfortable bed back home and how desperately tired I now felt, and then I reminded myself that this was God's work, and I rejoiced that even in my later years I was still able to do something for God.

What a joy and a tremendous privilege!

How did this work start? Well, let me go back to the beginning.

CHAPTER 1

Beginnings

The first time I met Alan was at a church youth club; at least, that's when he first noticed me. We did not actually meet. Apparently we had been in a group talking and I had jumped back in excitement over something or other and landed on his toes.

What I didn't know at the time was that he had just come out of hospital after having his large toenails removed! It must have been so painful for him, but he never said a word - not audibly, anyway.

The next time our paths crossed was when I was panicking because I needed to be home by 9.30 pm. My father was extremely strict and I would be punished if I was late. Although I knew this, I always seemed to stay on longer than I should at one of the many meetings I attended in the church, and did not leave myself enough time to get home, which meant I always ended up taking my shoes off and running home in my stockinged feet. My mother often used to put the clock back so that I would not incur my father's wrath!

On this occasion one of the older girls said, "Don't worry, I'll ask Alan Penrose to take you home in his car. I'm sure he won't mind." So Alan kindly dropped me home and that was that.

During the drive home I said that I didn't know him and hadn't seen him at church or at any of the meetings before. He explained that he had worked in Port Talbot but had now opened a business in Cardiff and had difficulty getting to any mid-week meetings. He also spent weekends in Port Talbot and just came to church when he was able.

A few months later I was late again and Alan, seeing me fly out the door, asked if he could help by giving me a lift. I was so grateful and thanked him profusely as I arrived home again just in time.

I belonged to the church choir and we practised every Tuesday evening. I enjoyed those evenings very much. However, my father wondered if that was where I was really going, and I discovered that he had checked with the choirmaster on a number of occasions to see if I had really been there. I think he thought that maybe I was meeting a member of the opposite sex. Even though I was sixteen, he felt that he needed to keep a strict watch over me. He was probably right!

One Tuesday evening I came out to walk home to find Alan sitting outside in his car. He wound down the window and asked me if I would like a lift home. I laughed, "No, I'm fine tonight, thank you. I'm actually in good time."

"Well, jump in anyway," he said, "It will save you walking."

So I did, and that is how our courtship began.

By now, I had become a Christian. Alan was also a Christian. Although I was young and obviously had much to learn about the Christian life and what it meant to be a real disciple, I can say looking back, with certainty, that the Lord truly put us together.

Getting to know Alan better increased my admiration for him. His father had died when he was twelve years old leaving his mother to bring up four children on her own. He had aspirations to be a teacher and was doing well at the grammar school. However, during the summer holidays he had gone to help his uncle who ran a greengrocer's shop in

Port Talbot. He had come back to Cardiff when the holidays had finished only to inform his mother that he was now going to help his uncle in the business in Port Talbot.

This distressed his mother. She felt that it was a waste of his education. The three older children had all gone to grammar school and had done well in their chosen professions. She tried to persuade him that he was making a mistake, but no method she employed could change his mind. His determination was already in evidence. Nothing or nobody could move him and so he started work in Port Talbot.

Although he worked hard and enjoyed the business, he was unhappy with some aspects of the work and after only six months decided to return to Cardiff and branch out on his own. He was still going to Port Talbot on the weekends because he had a girlfriend there. My appearance on the scene ended that relationship. What part my ability to carry sacks of potatoes had on his decision he did not disclose. But we did fall in love with each other as well.

On his return, he got a driving job delivering bread and did that work for three months in order to save enough money to buy himself an old bus. He then ripped the seats out and put in a counter and shelves and was ready to start his own mobile greengrocer round. He had a ready-made route based on the bread round and so he had started in business, using the garage at the back of his mother's house to store the bus, and the middle room to store the groceries.

I now had a job, but Saturday was my day off and I used to go out on the bus with Alan and help him. At the end of the day I received my wages, a bar of Turkish Delight (it was my favourite - obviously I worked for love, not money!). As we drove from street to street, I would sit on an orange box at the side of Alan until we got to the next stop. How I enjoyed those Saturdays; they were hard work, but I loved being with Alan and enjoyed meeting so many different people. It was a real education for me.

We became engaged in the face of opposition from my father saying that eighteen years of age was far too young. When he discovered that Alan had already bought the ring he was left with very little option. He must have felt he had the last word when he informed me that I could not get married until I was twenty-one.

The engagement party was hardly a success for the simple reason that we were not there. We were particularly busy on the mobile that day, not arriving home until midnight. We found that not only had all the people gone but the food as well. Some engagement party!

I had, of course, by now got to know Alan's mother. She was a lovely Christian and I admired her so much, despite the fact that when I first met her she persistently called me by the name of Alan's former girlfriend! She helped Alan load the mobile shop and worked so hard, often well into the evening. Alan was the youngest son and they were very fond of each other. Looking back, I often wonder how she felt when I suddenly came on the scene. She never once showed any resentment and always treated me with so much love and care. Although she had four children, when a cousin's wife died in childbirth leaving a baby and three other children, she took them all in and looked after them, keeping the baby on and bringing her up with her own family. She had had a hard life in so many ways but constantly thanked God for His goodness to her. I was very fond of her.

It seems strange now looking back, especially to the Saturdays that we worked, to think we could go out at nine o'clock in the morning and not arrive home sometimes until gone midnight. In those days people waited for us to come well into the night, often sitting on the wall with their baskets ready. Alan and I would take it in turns to run out and knock the doors.

A lot of our round was on a council estate and we met many different characters. One lady was delightful, but she was a real rogue. She even collected money for a wreath for her husband who had died. The trouble was he was still very much alive! She would always want things 'on the book,' and one day, knowing I had not been well, she said, "I want to buy a bunch of flowers." She chose them and gave them to me saying, "Put them on the book, Al." For all that, you could not help but like her. Another time she really gave Alan the rough edge of her tongue. We had had a row on the bus and I had thrown my engagement ring at him. It landed in the loose potatoes we carried and we spent ages looking for it. "You look after that girl," she said, "or I won't be coming on your bus anymore." She was just one of the many interesting characters I still remember so well.

By now Alan could afford to have a mobile shop custom-made and how proud he was when it finally came! It was luxurious after the last one, although it was sad saying goodbye to the old bus. It was over eight metres in length and I also drove this one, but getting it in and out of the garage was quite a feat as the space at the rear of the garage was very limited. However, neither of us ever bumped it, although I did once bring down the telephone wires in one street.

Alan now heard about a shop that was for sale and we went to see it. It was on the same estate where we were running the mobile shop. It was in a terrible state. The owner had lost a leg, and his interest in the business had vanished altogether. We knew that we could make something of it and Alan was keen to buy it. There was only one snag; above the shop were living quarters and the council would only allow a married couple to run the shop and live there.

"We're going to have to get married," Alan said.

"But my father will never let me," I replied. "After all, he said I couldn't get married until I am twenty-one and I'm only eighteen and a half!"

"We will have to explain about the shop and persuade him to change his mind," was Alan's response.

My poor father obviously felt pushed into a corner once again and, I think reluctantly, agreed that we could get married. I got married two weeks after my nineteenth birthday.

Our plan now was that Alan should continue running the mobile, while I ran the shop. When the shop got on its feet he would give up the mobile and we would run the shop together. So we started. Our two mums also came to work there and together with some staff, we were able to get the shop up and running. Again, things were so different in those days, with customers queuing outside the shop on a Saturday morning waiting for others to come out so that they could be served. I thrived on the hard work and enjoyed it so much.

I was young, and after we closed in the night, I often used to get lonely and a bit scared above the shop on my own, waiting for Alan to come in from his round. I would then ring my dear mother-in-law who would chat to me for a while, and then she would always say, "Remember you are not on your own. God is right there with you." She was such a blessing to me at that time.

After a few years, I found that I was expecting our first child. We were delighted, but of course I still had to run the shop. I vividly remember constantly having to excuse myself while serving a customer because of the interruptions of morning sickness, and then come back and carry on serving. It was not made easy, either, by the fact that the bananas came in long, heavy wooden boxes and the potatoes in large hessian sacks. There was a lot of heavy lifting.

Rubbish constantly had to be taken to the local tip and Alan fixed up a cushion for me so that I could still drive our van without the steering wheel getting in the way of my ever-expanding stomach. I was actually at the tip when I went into labour but managed to get home between the pains.

That St David's day saw the birth of our first child, a boy, and it was not long before I was back at work, with the pram parked outside the shop. Two years later his brother was born. We now had two very precious sons.

We were selling fresh pies now, so each morning very early I would put the baby in his carrycot in the back of the car and make my way to the local bakery where I would pick up the trays of hot pies. I was often in a hurry to get back because the baby was crying and can still remember Alan's voice as he opened the boot to get the pies out. "Oh no! Not again. You've squashed some of the pies." Of course, they were hot and still soft and when I had to brake, one had gone into the other.

By this time the shop was on its feet, so Alan sold the mobile and joined me there. That was not quite so easy because we each wanted to do things our own way. So we devised a plan where we each took charge of certain areas. Even so, when we worked late in the evening a bag of flour or such-like would often fly through the air as we lost patience with each other. We then had to spend the next half an hour or so cleaning up the mess. Well, we were young then, and foolish!

The Lord often uses past experiences in preparing us for future work. Getting up early, working late at night, lifting heavy loads, driving long hours, working under all kinds of pressures and dealing with all kinds of people. Little did we know that God was fitting us for our Romanian adventure!

CHAPTER 2

Romania via Vietnam

After running the business for thirty years, we felt that although we had not reached retiring age, it was time to sell up and move on. It had been hard work, but we had enjoyed it immensely. Supermarkets were beginning to open and we felt that things were changing. We now wanted to serve the Lord in some more specific way. Would He be able to use us at our age, we wondered? Would there be some work that we could do for Him? We should have known that the Lord had His plans for us.

I had been led into working with the Vietnamese boat people who had escaped to Britain from their country which at that time had a very severe regime. The Lord had given me a compassion for these dear people and I had become involved in collecting goods and furniture for the homes that had been allocated to them in and around Cardiff. A local removal firm loaned me their lorry and a driver, and each Saturday, together with young people from our church, we spent the whole day collecting things and taking them to a warehouse that had also been loaned, free of charge.

The first thing we did when we knew which families were coming was to go to the warehouse to pick up the furniture that was needed for their particular house. Alan and I usually did this late at night because we were so busy during the day, and we had to shine the headlights of the van into the warehouse as it had no electricity. Once loaded, the van then had to be taken to the various houses and the local church would start looking after their particular family. It was really hard work.

At the same time we were given a family of our own, so as well as furnishing the house that they were given, we had the responsibility, with our church, of looking after them. This family consisted of eleven persons and we did all that we could to make the house warm and homely for them. When they arrived my heart went out to them. They had been through so much and the Lord gave me such a love for them which has continued until this day.

Then began the practicalities of introducing them to their new way of life. They had to register with the local doctor and they all badly needed dental treatment. They needed to know how to shop and to get to know the currency. There were a thousand and one things which took up much time. But what a joy it was to see these dear friends slowly, ever so slowly, settle in!

It was very much an ordinary practical work, but later on in my dealings with the family, and with future events in my life, the Lord showed me that when we do the ordinary things in obedience to Him, He then does the supernatural, as He did with Peter when he walked on the water. It was when Peter got out of the boat in practical obedience that the Lord did the supernatural and he walked on the water!

The first experience of this was when I took the family to the Christian Mission Ship, *The Doulos*. They had escaped from Vietnam in a boat and I thought it would be good for them to see this large ship which was so fully equipped. I wondered what they would make of it. They still spoke hardly any English but we were getting by wonderfully with actions and sign language. They understood what I had tried to convey to them and agreed to come.

While we were looking around the ship, a young oriental man approached me and asked if the family were from China or Vietnam. I explained that they were Chinese but had lived in Vietnam from where they had escaped.

"May I speak to them?" he asked.

"Of course," I replied.

"The only thing is I don't speak Cantonese, only a local dialect, Tertu. What language or dialect do they speak?"

Well, of course, I had heard them speak but didn't have any idea whether it was Mandarin, Cantonese or whatever. So the young man said, "Well, I'll speak to them in Tertu but it is unlikely that it will be their dialect."

He approached them and started to speak. I watched their expressions change as slowly their faces lit up and they started talking excitedly.

The young man turned to me and said, "This is amazing. I am the only Chinese on this ship and it was my day off today, but I changed days with my friend because he needed to go somewhere. I feel this is of God and would like with your permission to share the gospel with your friends and show them some slides."

I hesitated, as I had simply brought the family to see the ship, nothing more. I did not want to abuse their trust in me and lead them to think that I had brought them here to thrust my 'religion' on them. That was the furthest thing from my mind. The young man was gently persistent. "I really believe this is of the Lord," he urged. So very reluctantly I gave him permission, feeling very uncomfortable.

They sat down and he stood in front of them obviously sharing the gospel, complete with slides.

The family listened intently. At the end he turned to me and said, "I am now going to ask them if they would like to give their lives to Christ."

"Oh, no!" I thought, "This is even worse!"

I watched as the mother and father put their hands up. The young man turned to me. "The mother and father have indicated that they wish to receive Christ." At this point I felt I ought to speak to them before matters went any further, so I asked the young man if he would interpret for me. He readily agreed.

I told them how much I cared for them, how God had indeed led me to look after them, but that I had not brought them to the ship to talk about my 'religion'. I had no idea that the young man was going to be there and that I did not want them to accept Jesus just because of their love for me.

The young man translated this. When he had finished speaking the father stood up and spoke fervently. The young man turned to me. "The father has said they understand perfectly what you have said and thank you, but they still want to accept Christ." So he led them in a prayer of repentance and they received Christ into their hearts.

On the way home I prayed silently, "Lord, I am still uneasy about this situation. Will You give me a sign so that I would truly know that this is of You?" I did not have to wait long. When we arrived back at their house, the mother and father took from their necks the charms which had been under their clothes and which I did not know they had been wearing. They threw them in the open fire and said with fervour – "JESUS NOW!"

Over the following years nearly all of the family became Christians. The Lord led each one in a different way. The mother and father attend the local Chinese church and others are in other churches in Cardiff. The mother and father have even been to France evangelizing among their own people. God is so good.

As Alan was now free from the demands of business, a friend of ours who was involved in a ministry for the Jewish people in Poland asked if he would accompany him on these journeys. So Alan started going to and from Poland by van, supporting him in this very important work. These were dangerous days in Poland, and they had many difficult moments but the Lord protected them. In turn, after my work with our Vietnamese friends had become easier, I had been led in a remarkable way into running *The Olive Branch,* which was a Christian coffee shop and bookshop in our village and which was part of the work of the local Baptist church. We both knew that we were engaged in work to which the Lord had called us and were satisfied to know that we were both in His will.

Everyone in *The Olive Branch* worked voluntarily, and as a result we were able to give thousands of pounds away both at home and abroad to needy causes. Those who could not actually work there gave their time in other ways, such as cleaning the windows, washing the teacloths, and cooking at home. We had 78 ladies cooking for *The Olive Branch*. We even had an excellent mention in the food column of the *Guardian*.

The lady who wrote the column had come to visit her aunt in Rhiwbina and had come to *The Olive Branch* for a meal. She was so surprised to see that the church could do something of such a high standard that she wrote a full page spread in the *Guardian*, complete with a photograph of all the food. I was able, through the interview, to share why we did it and whom we were serving; what an honour to speak about God's work in the *Guardian*! A lady from the BBC's *Woman's Hour* also came to the shop to interview me as well as the customers, asking them why they liked coming to *The Olive Branch*. These were indeed "famous moments."

I so enjoyed running the coffee shop. I was working ten hours each day - that was my responsibility, and it gave me so much joy. It was hard work, but being a greengrocer's wife I was used to that and it was wonderful to see God at work there. How amazingly He arranged for certain people to sit next to each other on the tables and how remarkably He guided conversations!

One such arrangement I have never forgotten to this day. It was a busy lunch hour and there was a long queue, which was usual. There was just one place left on the back table that held four people. I went through the queue looking for one person who was alone and found one man near the end. I told him there was one place free out in the back room if he did not mind sharing. He said that was fine and took the place. I continued back and fore waiting on the different tables and noticed that he and the other three people were getting on well and were deep in conversation. However, that was not unusual as *The Olive Branch* was a very friendly place and this often happened.

We were very busy, and when I next passed the table he had gone. The other three people were still there however, and called me over.

"Something amazing has just happened," they declared. "The gentleman that you put on our table was a Jew and for a long time he had been wondering whether Jesus could possibly be his longed-for Messiah."

"And...?" I said, not quite understanding what they were trying to convey.

"Well, we three are converted Jews and we were able to share with him about Jesus and how He *was* the Messiah."

I felt such a wonder and a joy within me, words of praise bubbled on my lips; I felt almost overcome by emotion. What a wonderful God we have! He is a God of every individual situation. He arranged for that dear man to be in the right place in that queue at the right time and arranged for that one place on the table to be empty. Coincidence? Of course not! It was God at work, and later, as He called both Alan and me to our present work, I was to see Him at work in this way over and over again.

So, I carried on with *The Olive Branch* work that He had given me, loving every minute of it.

While Alan continued working in Poland, travelling back and forth, he had also become involved with the Romanian Missionary Society (RMS). He had met Pastor Josef Ton, a Romanian pastor who had been exiled to America and who was visiting Britain. He had said what a desperate need there was to train men to become pastors in Romania. There were a few theological colleges open, but only two or three students were allowed through each year. This was so that the communist regime could say that they did have theological colleges that were open and running. However, it was just a façade to keep the West happy.

Josef explained that he believed with all his heart that the communist government would one day fall and then leaders would be needed to lead churches, Bible schools, and Christian universities. His plan was to train suitable men in secret in Romania. The qualified lecturers from this country would go to Romania as tourists and meet up secretly with these men who would have already received study material that had been smuggled in on microfiche - the microfiche readers having already been taken in. Alan caught Josef's vision and so became a member of the RMS team organizing and working for Josef's vision from this country. Little did he realize that this was all part of God's plan, when He would one day give him a very special ministry of his own.

Both of us had become very busy in our own ways. What had happened to taking it easier when we retired?

In 1990 Josef's vision came into being and the Romanian regime fell. Almost immediately the RMS received many phone calls from Christian contacts in Romania asking for help. They were desperate for so many things, and so within three weeks of the revolution Alan and his co-driver were on their way to Romania with a lorry full of aid. What a hard journey that was, having to get to Romania and then negotiate his way around the country, but what a blessing and a privilege to be able to go!

Alan was to make three more aid journeys under the auspices of the RMS before the money that had come in for these journeys finished. The RMS had money, of course, but that was for the teaching programme, and obviously could not be spent on aid, no matter how much that was needed.

However, Alan had become very concerned. He could see that there was such a great need for help in so many places in Romania. His friend's work in Poland had now come to an end and Alan's services were no longer required. The RMS took only a little of his time as he was part of a team. Could he help in any way? We discussed the situation and prayed about this desperate need that we could see was clearly there and came to the conclusion that we should set up a charity enabling us to take trucks of aid into Romania. We decided to call the charity simply *Support for Romania*. It was left to Alan to sort out the renting of the trucks. At this point he had many contacts who were willing to supply things that were needed there, and Alan set off with the friend whom he had helped with his Polish work.

God was opening a door before us, and the years were to prove that it was not to be shut.

CHAPTER 3

God Calls Me

Whilst Alan was doing those journeys for the RMS I was still working at *The Olive Branch*. However, for a year I had had this strange feeling inside that my work there was going to come to an end. I did not want it to. I had been there six and a half years and loved it so much I would have stayed another six and a half years. However, the feeling did not go away and I remember thinking that maybe the Lord was very gently preparing me for something that He knew would be so difficult for me - to finish working there. But I had to be absolutely sure. *The Olive Branch* was running smoothly and if He was indeed preparing me to come out I needed to hear His voice say so very, very, clearly.

One Sunday morning while Alan was away in Romania, I decided to go to the local Elim church for the morning service. It was a church where I had learnt much, before happily settling in my local Baptist church and I really felt this urge to go there again that morning. Because I was not sure what time it started, I arrived early. I had to sit outside in the car for about half an hour. I prayed during this time, "Lord, I am in a strange place. If You want to speak to me with regards to *The Olive Branch*, I want You to know that I am open and listening. If You choose not to, Lord, I will wait until You do. I do not move a step until I hear Your voice clearly."

I entered the church and took a seat almost at the back.

There was a word given that was for the church; the hymns and choruses were beautiful, but none of the words seemed appropriate to me. The sermon was about marriage and was a tremendous help and encouragement, but did not apply to my situation.

When we came to the time of communion, the bread was passed around and then the wine and I held the glass waiting for the minister to say the familiar words. He stepped forward and said, "The Lord has given me a word for a lady who is here this morning. She has sat through the service and has already told the Lord that she is open and listening for His voice." These were the very words that I had used to the Lord when I was in the car. My heart started to thump and I could feel my hand shaking as I held the glass.

The minister continued, "This is what the Lord would say to You. What you have felt in your heart He would confirm to be true. He is asking you to set aside the work to which He called you, for He has a new work for you to do. Do not be afraid to put this work on one side for it is His work and it is in His hands." He went on to say some other very precious things that were such an encouragement to me. I felt so loved and blessed, I started to cry.

The service meanwhile carried on with me sniffling through the tears running down my cheeks. "Lord, You have spoken to me. You have shown me my work has indeed come to an end but You have also shown how much You love and care for me. Lord, thank You, thank You." However, on the way home I started to think what this would mean.

How could I now return to *The Olive Branch* knowing that I would have to leave? How I would miss the customers; how sad I would feel as I told them all that my work was finished there!   I honestly did not think I could cope. How I loved the work, especially the customers, and it was such a rewarding and worthwhile ministry! Nevertheless, no matter how good the work is it is pointless if you know that is not where the Lord wants you to be. So I knew that I would have to make my plans to leave not knowing what my new work was to be.

I was sad that Alan was still away because I wanted to share straightaway what had happened, so I drove to a friend's house and shared it with her. She understood immediately what a wrench this was going to be for me. I had been in *The Olive Branch* now six and a half years and it was going to be hard to let it go. We prayed together and then I returned home, anxiously waiting for Alan's return. He returned safely and recounted all that had transpired during the journey and then, as usual, he said, "How about you, everything alright - any news?"

"Yes, I have news." I slowly explained to him just what had happened, sharing with him my thoughts about not going back to *The Olive Branch*. I had injured my back and was due to return after a few weeks away. I think too, at this point, I was afraid that if I re-immersed myself in the work, I might not hear the Lord's voice when He spoke to me about the new work. Also, would I be open to hearing Him? I could not afford to take that chance, after He had spoken to me so clearly. I dared not stay.

With a sigh of relief, I knew that Alan understood perfectly and he advised me to go and see the senior elder at the church as soon as I could. So I gave him a ring and arranged to see him and his wife the next morning.

Howard and Gwen were dear friends of ours and they had always been such a loving support as I sought to carry out the Lord's work in the coffee shop. I knew that my leaving was going to create a big hole there. There was a lady working alongside me who stepped in when needed, but would she be prepared to take over? Howard and Gwen knew as well as I did the many practicalities of running the coffee shop. They also knew how much I loved being there, but would they now understand why I felt that I wanted to leave straightaway? I need not have worried. They did understand and with their blessing, and Gwen's assurance that she would explain the situation to everyone, I relinquished my work at *The Olive Branch*.

About a month after I had finished in the coffee shop Alan was due to go to Romania and he suggested that, as the Lord had not yet shown me the 'new' work, I could go along with him to help. He needed a driver for one of the lorries and an extra pair of hands. He was by now taking convoys of lorries over with aid.

I readily agreed. It was something that I could do to help him, although I knew it would be hard and I hoped that I would cope alright. I made up my mind that with the Lord's help I would - I would not in any way let Alan down.

So, I embarked on my first journey to Romania. It took us three days to get to the border of Romania. When we did, I could hardly take in all that I saw.

The road was not much more than a dirt track. The guards at the border had grubby uniforms on. They were smoking, talking among themselves and even coming to the windows of the vehicles asking in turn for cigarettes, beer, coke, chocolate and bonbons (sweets). Everything just seemed a shambles. There were Gypsies and many other people, one who looked extremely poor, either just standing or sitting on the side of the road. I could not believe this was supposed to be the actual crossing into Romania

Standing beside the truck I looked at my watch. It was 2 o'clock in the morning and twenty degrees below freezing. We had been there three hours, waiting to enter Romania. Our papers were correct but the border guards were just being awkward. Apparently this was usual.

"What", I asked myself, "is a fifty-year-old woman doing here?"

I thought of my comfortable bed back home, and how desperately tired I now felt. And then I reminded myself that this was God's work, and I rejoiced that even in my later years I was still able to do something for God.

What a joy and a tremendous privilege!

Because of the inefficiency and the laid-back attitude it was many hours before we finally crossed the border and entered Romania. Did anybody know what they were supposed to be doing, I asked myself? But at last, we were actually here! There were many youngsters lining the road from the border. They all looked at us and seemed to be blowing kisses in our direction. I remarked to Alan later how sweet that was, only to be told that they were not blowing kisses but asking for cigarettes!

As we entered Romania it was as if I was entering a different world. I was astonished at how dirty everything was and how terribly, terribly drab. The few shops that we passed on the way to our destination were dimly lit and the windows dirty and dusty with just a few items on show. The apartment blocks looked as if they were about to collapse at any moment and were again so very dirty.

I could hardly believe that we were driving along a main road. It was like a rough cart track, with large potholes here and there and open sewers which were indicated by small branches placed inside them. Then there were horses and carts, many carrying families all huddled together in the back with old, tattered blankets around them. The people who were walking around looked so poorly-dressed and I noted that each one carried an old linen bag. I discovered later that people always carried these even if they were going to work, just in case on the way they spotted some food that had come into a shop that day!

What upset me were the faces of these dear people. They looked so careworn, so sad, so weighed down with worries. They had no spring in their step but trudged along, their eyes downcast, as though they carried the weight of the whole world on their shoulders. My heart went out to these shuffling figures who seemed to have no hope or purpose. This is what Ceausescu and his regime had done for these people. He, together with his wife, had ruled the country with a rod of iron. His people had been persecuted, starved and oppressed, whilst he and his wife had lived lives of luxury. He had demolished seventeen districts in Bucharest in order to build separate palaces for himself and his wife. His people's homes and livelihoods were destroyed so that he might live in indescribable opulence. His palace alone had 1800 rooms and his wife's palace was being built five hundred yards away!

I returned from that first trip to Romania very humbled. I realized how much we take for granted living in this country. We had stayed with Christians in their homes and I had witnessed first hand how much they loved the Lord, how strong their faith was, even though they had so very little by our standards. I had been moved at how full many churches were that we had visited. By full, I mean standing in the aisles, and outside on the pavement.

I had spoken to a young girl of about fifteen after one service. She spoke English and I told her how amazed I had been to see the churches so full, whereas the churches in our country are often empty. She looked at me and said, "Ah, but in the West you have too many things that take your eyes off God." Sadly, I had to concede that it was true.

The people of Romania were so hospitable. They had given us all that they had, which had often been very little. People had slept on the floor and given us their beds. I came home thanking God for my learning experience.

A couple of months later, Alan was off to Romania again and as the Lord still had not revealed to me the new work that He had for me, I agreed to go and help him a second time. I again found it hard physically and yet again so rewarding. We were able to meet people's needs and show them that they were not forgotten by us and, more importantly, not forgotten by God.

It was towards the end of this journey that the Lord spoke to me so very clearly. Not in an audible voice, but it was His voice that I knew and loved and recognized speaking to my spirit. "This is the new work that I have given you to do, to work alongside Alan encouraging and supporting him."

I was totally shocked. Strange as it may seem, this had never even entered my mind and yet I knew that the Lord had truly spoken to me. My heart sank. This was not the sort of work I had envisaged at all and furthermore, I was not sure that I wanted to or could work with Alan – or, for that matter that he could work with me.

In our Christian lives, all the work we had done for the Lord had been done separately and that suited us both. As much as we loved each other and respected the other's work, we knew from experience that we could not work together. Even when we had our business, we worked in different areas. We each worked in such a different way that when we had tried to work together it was always a disaster and now this was what the Lord was asking me to do. It would never work. I told the Lord this, to which He calmly replied, "It will work because I am in it."

"All right, Lord. It is not the work I would have chosen, but You have spoken to me clearly. My desire is only to please You. Now please be with me as I break the 'happy' news to Alan."

A couple of days later we were sat having breakfast when I told Alan that I had something to say to him. He put down the paper and looked at me questioningly. I had prepared carefully in my mind what I was going to say, but all of that went by the board as I found myself blurting out, "I now know the new work that the Lord has called me to do. I believe He is asking me to work alongside you in *Support For Romania*, for me to be a support and encouragement to you."

I would like to say that Alan threw his arms around me saying how wonderful that was and that he was delighted. Instead he looked startled. Then his face fell.

"Are you sure? I mean, you could have made a mistake couldn't you?"

I looked him straight in the eyes. "Alan. Ask yourself one question, would I want to work with you?"

He looked at me and the reply came back, "No, you would not and neither would I like particularly to work with you."

"Exactly! That is one of the reasons why I know it's of the Lord."

"Ann, it will never work. For a start you are far too bossy."

"Me, bossy? You're the bossy one. I can remember when ..."

And so we had an argument as to who was the bossy one!

At the end we just looked wearily at each other and smiled.

"Alan," I said "I have got good news as well. The Lord has told me it will work because He is in it - so that is a real encouragement, isn't it?" Alan took my hands in his. "It is, and the work is already growing quite quickly. I could do with help." So we sat at the kitchen table and committed ourselves and the work into His hands.

As we opened our eyes after praying, Alan looked at me nervously, "When do you want to start?"

"How about tomorrow?" I said equally nervously, "We may as well start straight away."

"I suppose so," said Alan, giving a huge sigh, which I felt was completely unnecessary!

I was very apprehensive the next day as I reported to Alan for duty. I was determined that I was not going to try and take over in order to do things my way. The Lord had called me to be a support and encouragement and that was what I was determined to be.

Many people by now were sending gifts of money to support the work and there were letters of enquiries among the correspondence that had to be acknowledged. Alan had been doing this on his typewriter. Now, as I stood in his office, he presented me with a pile of unanswered correspondence saying, "Well, you can start on these. I thought actually it would be good for you to do all the letters in future." I bit my lip as my heart sank. Oh, no, not this. I hated writing letters. I knew that usually in a marriage the wife wrote the letters, remembered birthdays and did the Christmas cards, but we were unusual in that, with us, it was the reverse. Alan did all that - I absolutely hated writing cards and letters. I took them in my hand and turned to go out of the office, resisting the urge to throw them at Alan as he said, "Come on, smile. I know how much you enjoy writing letters." I sat down at the kitchen table looking at the pile of papers before me, tears in my eyes. I had to take this to the Lord. I could not cope with this and this was the *first* job. After I had spoken to Him about it I felt a great peace come over me and also the very powerful impression that instead of typing the letters I should do them by hand. I began to feel very positive at the thought of people being pleased to receive a handwritten letter in this day and age and how I could make each letter meaningful.

Nearly eighteen years later I am still writing the letters by hand and enjoying this part of the work so much. Sometimes, because of my packing at the warehouse, I get behind with the letters and they pile up. I had 62 letters on one occasion but even then I enjoyed writing each one - I truly did. Considering my past record, I knew that I had been given a gift from God.

CHAPTER 4

After Ceausescu

Romania is in so many ways a beautiful country. The Carpathian Mountains are reminiscent of Switzerland and travelling over them is truly awe inspiring, with fir- studded slopes and many mountain streams.

The people are so creative and their craftwork is second to none. If only other things were in order, it could be a great tourist attraction. People who do go to Romania on holiday usually visit Brasov or the Black Sea area which caters for tourists. Brasov is particularly good for those wanting a skiing holiday. However, the rest of the country is in a bad way with roads and hotels in poor condition. There is little else, seemingly, to attract people, to bring revenue into the country.

The one name everyone associates with Romania is Ceausescu, whose palace in Bucharest stands as a monument to one man's evil, and as I mentioned in the last chapter, much was demolished to build this and a palace for his wife. All this while his people were living in abject poverty.

Here are some statistics:-

There are 1,800 rooms in the palace, with 1,200 chandeliers (one   weighing 4 tons).

For five years 24,000 workers toiled in three shifts 24 hours a day.

Ceausescu and his wife made daily tours while it was being built.   One day they did not like the way a 60-foot marble staircase was built and had it demolished.

One of the hallways is longer than any London Underground station.

Fifteen Districts were demolished to make room for the building which covers 1,000,000 square feet and is 280 feet high.

Underneath the palace was an Olympic-size athletics stadium used as a car park which was full of Ceausescu's cars.

Seven hundred architects were used.

Materials used in the construction included:-

    a) seven hundred train-loads of marble.

    b) entire forests of elm, oak and sweet cherry.

    c) two million tons of sand.

    d) half a million tons of cement.

    e) three and a half thousand tons of crystal and leather.

    f) Gold and silver threads for the curtains.

This reminds us of the story in the Bible where the man built bigger barns in order to contain his vast wealth. Little did he know that that night his soul would be required of him. And, of course, Ceausescu's people rose up against him until finally, after a short trial, he and his wife were shot.

We are often asked what it is like in Romania now over seventeen years after the revolution. It is tough and we feel that little progress has been made in a really beneficial way. Yes, there are more goods in the shops now, but most of the items are at western prices and the average wage is twenty pounds per week. We are told that many families have only bread on the table and we can believe that.

Many people cannot afford to pay their gas or electricity bills. If one person in a block of apartments does not pay his bill the whole block gets cut off. The central heating is usually controlled from a central source. It is often on full blast in the summer and off in the winter, with many families sending young children to their grandparents in the villages where they have wood burning stoves. The roads are worse than ever, the main roads full of open sewers, open manholes and uneven surfaces.

At night in the country areas it is so difficult to drive because of the horses and carts which are travelling without any lights – unless, of course, the man is holding out a cigarette lighter in his hand as his means of lighting and you can imagine what good that is. You really cannot see them until you are right on top of them. Vehicles are also in a poor state of repair and one wonders how they manage to keep some of them on the road. The occasional bus that you see is invariably filthy dirty and yet has curtains hanging at the windows. It is normal to see a car being repaired in the middle of the road and men who are drunk lying in the road also. One of our lorries passed a man on a bicycle who was obviously drunk and wobbling all over the place, so he had been given a wide berth. A few miles up the road the driver was stopped by the police who said that the man had been lying in the road and that the lorry had knocked him off his bicycle. They confiscated the driver's passport and it took the help of Romanian friends and a couple of days' wasted time before it was returned.

Many of the police, but not all, of course, are corrupt themselves. We have experienced this over and over again. Once we were travelling along a main road when we were stopped and told that lorries were prohibited from travelling on that road. We knew that this was not true. We had been on this road many times and anyway, other lorries were still flying past us. They had seen a British lorry and thought they could make some easy money, for they were demanding twenty dollars. We refused. The officer asked us a few times and we still refused. He then changed his tactics.

"Beer?"

"No, we don't drink."

"Cigarettes?"

"No, we don't smoke."

"Coca-Cola?"

"No."

"Bonbons?" (sweets)

"No."

"Chocolate?"

"No."

With a resigned look he slammed our door shut and motioned us to travel on.

On another occasion we had just drawn out of a lay-by and the police pulled us up. "Radar speeding," the policeman said. It was so ludicrous we laughed. "Don't be ridiculous," we said, "we've only just pulled out."

"Radar," he repeated determinedly. "Fifty dollars."

"I'm not paying, and that's that," said Alan. "I have never heard anything so ridiculous." The policeman then went through the usual list, beer, cigarettes, Coca-Cola, bonbons. Again, realizing he was not getting anywhere he let us go, and this was repeated on many other occasions. I have to say that unfortunately there is a lot of corruption still in Romania. It seems to be everywhere. I remember once that I was desperate to go to the toilet when we came to a garage. I jumped down from the lorry and ran towards the toilet, which was outside. As I did so a huge, burly lady barred my path holding out her hand. "Toilet tax," she demanded. I tried to push past her, but she would not let me pass. "Toilet tax," she reiterated. I ran back to the lorry and told Alan that I was not being allowed to use the toilet and she was asking for toilet tax of all things.

"What!" he exploded. "Come back with me." So I followed sheepishly behind him.

"My wife is going to the toilet and she is not paying any toilet tax," he said. Then to me, "Right, go to the toilet." I scuttled past her while Alan stood with his arms folded waiting for me to come out!

The health service, as a whole in Romania, is pretty appalling. We can hardly believe the things that we see in these hospitals; toilets that are filthy and have no seats or lids; bins with bloodied bandages spilling out into the corridors along with many other unspeakable things; and the smell is something else. Many of the hospitals have lifts operated by an old man or woman sitting inside, usually smoking. I always say to Alan, "If I'm taken ill in Romania just get me home quickly, I don't want to go into hospital here." There is a lot of AIDS in the country because the same needles are used over and over again simply because they do not have enough needles or syringes

There are often two people in a bed, because of the shortage of beds, and we have also seen patients wearing hats, gloves, scarves and coats in bed because there is no heating. And we complain about our health service! We have also seen hospital bedding outside the hospitals hanging over the fence to dry. It was snowing heavily at the time.

Amongst the horror stories we could recount, one concerns a friend of ours who needed a gall bladder operation but did not have the money to pay. The doctor said to him, "I understand that you are a carpenter."

"Yes," replied our friend.

"I will give you a picture of a piece of furniture I would like." responded the doctor. "Go home and make it for me, and I will do your operation."

Another friend in Ploesti nearly lost her life because she had a Caesarean operation and badly needed blood. She had to refuse, knowing that a lot of the blood in that area was contaminated. It was only prayer that brought her through. We actually saw in a travel brochure for Romania, "If you are ill, quit the country quick."

One of our drivers broke his arm falling off a lorry and had to have it set in Romania without anaesthetic because they did not have any. However, when he returned home he had to have it re-set because they had made such a bad job of it.

I remember one day we were at a pastor's house about to go to church when his wife fell and put her arm through a window. She severed an artery, a tourniquet was quickly put on her and someone telephoned for an ambulance. It still had not come after fifteen minutes so the pastor rushed her to the local hospital in his car. Another fifteen minutes later we heard a loud ringing bell and thought at last it has come, but a bit late. However, it was not an ambulance that turned up but an antiquated fire engine. There was no ambulance available.

God provided beforehand for another friend who was expecting a baby. The child had been born by the time we returned on our next journey. Our friend shared with us that she had needed a caesarean section and had been asked for money before the doctor would perform the operation. Some money had been left for her by one of our party on our last visit. She had saved it "just in case" and so she was able to pay for the operation. Then she sat down and dissolved into tears. There were three others who needed a caesarean but they did not have the money to pay. "What happened?" we asked. Looking up, she said through her tears, "The babies died."

We visited another friend who was in hospital in Romania and as we went into the ward we noticed that her husband gave the person on the door a jar of coffee and two pounds of sugar – that allowed entry to see his wife.

As I said earlier, the Romanian health service leaves a lot to be desired.

The Romanian people themselves, we have found, are highly creative, intelligent and hospitable. Whatever home you visit they always want you to stop for a meal. No time is inconvenient for them. They delight to see you. We have so much to learn about true hospitality, and yet their lives can be extremely hard. We still see people in the countryside washing their clothes in the stream (in winter as well) and the ladies working in the fields alongside the men.

I enjoy travelling through the villages taking in the lovely smell of the wood- burning stoves, seeing people sitting outside their homes on wooden benches or chairs chatting, the geese and chickens roaming freely, and in early evening, the cows coming down the road, each one turning into its respective home. We often ask ourselves, "How do they know?" Sometimes there are small tables by the roadside where meagre produce is put out to sell. If we see radishes we usually stop - they are huge and absolutely delicious and so cheap for a big bundle. These people have been through so much at the hands of President Ceausescu. This is what makes them so stoical and able to survive.

It is interesting to see a funeral pass by when you are in the country. The body is often carried on the back of an open carriage, not in a coffin but just lying there surrounded by flowers. It is pulled by horses and the mourners follow on foot, sometimes walking many miles. It can seem pretty gruesome at first but you get used to it after a while.

We realize as we go back and forth to Romania how fortunate we are to be living in this country and also what a wasteful society we have become. A throwaway society in every sense of the word. It would not be right here to tell of some of the things that we have been given because we are so grateful for them, but we have certainly had our eyes opened.

Our children could not possibly understand the fact that there were children who had never seen things like a banana, which was so in 1990. We were given boxes of bananas to take over for our orphanage, but were told by the director that we would have to peel them before we took them in, otherwise they would eat them with the skins on, all because they had never seen a banana and would not consider that you had to peel it. How very sad when our children can have so many varieties of fruit here!

CHAPTER 5

God in the Warehouse

God's timing is always perfect. When we retired from our business, we rented out our shop. A number of people had been tenants over the years and managed reasonably well. However, with the shopping climate changing and three new supermarkets opening nearby, the present tenant had found that he could not make his business pay and had consequently left. But the Romanian work had now grown considerably and we needed a large storage area. What better place than our old shop and warehouse? It had an area of 2,000 square feet and seemed to be ideal. Of course, it meant that we would not now be receiving any rent from that property, which was part of our income, but we felt that it was right to use the premises and that we could therefore trust the Lord for our reduced finances. So we went ahead and moved into our old shop. This was now to be our warehouse. Eventually, we were to need even more storage space and now have another warehouse of 12,000 square feet, which has been loaned to us free of charge by a Christian brother with the work at heart.

By now, many people had heard of our work and were faithfully supporting us. I think the fact that we actually took the goods ourselves to the individual places that we were supporting and also that Alan and I had been going out speaking at many different places about the work, meant that people knew things were not being just left in a warehouse for random distribution over there. Also, as they got to know us personally, they felt drawn towards the people of Romania and our work amongst them. While we are aware of the vast needs in other parts of the world, our conviction remains that Romania is where God has called us

Going out speaking about our work also helps people to be aware of the many different needs that still exist in Romania. We really appreciate this part of the work - we so enjoy meeting people, not only talking about the practical aspects of our work but also sharing how we have seen God at work and how we have seen that He really is a God who knows and cares about each individual. We are invited to secular groups as well as churches and other Christian groups, and we share the same message. It is that God loves us, but also that He desires us to know and love Him.

I clearly remember the first time that we went out together to speak. Alan spoke first and introduced us. Then he said, "I have brought my wife along today also, and I will tell her when to speak." It was a ladies' meeting and I could at once sense their hostility. Alan did not actually mean it to come out that way, but they did not like it. However, I soon rectified the matter. As I got up to speak I quickly defused the situation by saying, "Well, ladies, he may tell me when I can speak but he won't be able to tell me when to stop."   They liked that!

At the same time the number of people on our mailing list was growing.   We were regularly sending out what we called our needs list (the list that is sent out to people on our mailing list for things that are needed for the next journey) a couple of months before we set out, together with an update of our work. Of course many others were drawn in by word of mouth and to date we now have over 1,300 people on our mailing list. We give times and dates when the warehouse is open to receive the goods, and then we have to sort and pack everything. Things that could not be delivered need to be picked up in our trusty van which also accompanies the trucks to Romania.

It is always such a tremendous joy for me to see the people turning up so faithfully at the warehouse on the days allocated, and we have made many friends over the years.

How we feel blessed by the things that people do for Romania - the elderly lady who is crippled with arthritis, but knits beautiful cardigans and jumpers for the children; the lady who stood and ironed thirty of her son's shirts which he did not want, even though she had a bad back. "There was nothing wrong with them," she said, "but I couldn't send them all crumpled up." Then there was the lady who hired a van (she had never driven one before) and came to us up the motorway from Wembley; the ladies who shared an eightieth birthday and decided that they would not give each other presents but wanted to express their joy of being blessed by the Lord over all those years and so presented us with a gift; and a group of ladies who meet once a week for tea, but instead of buying themselves cakes, they give their "cake money" for Romania.

We are now supported not only in and around Cardiff, but also from places much further afield, such as London, Norwich, Pembroke, Swindon, Weymouth and Worcester.

Sorting and packing in the warehouse provides a marvellous opportunity for fellowship among the team of ladies. They are from different churches and we all enjoy working together, sharing our joys and sorrows, as well as filling the boxes. We even have two ladies, twins (not young!) who deliver our mailing to local areas of Cardiff on their bicycles, saving us about sixty pounds in postage every time.

Alan also has men who faithfully come in to assist him with anything that needs to be moved and is heavy. Also, large donated items need to be collected in the van, and they help him organize the larger warehouse at Talbot Green.

We now have one man who supervises all the work that is needed to keep the vehicles on the road, another who organizes the collection of goods in our van, and another who does a lot of the computer work to keep our accounts in order.

There are two who check that all the computers we send out are in good working order; one lives in Telford and drives to Cardiff when needed. We also have a gentleman who is over eighty years young who comes to the warehouse each week and cuts up all the waste cardboard for us, stacking it in piles and tying it with string as well as clearing all the rubbish.

Two others check and repair all the bicycles that we receive. They have created their own workshop within the larger warehouse and every bicycle that is sent to Romania is in excellent condition. One of these men worked for Halfords until he retired. God certainly knows what He is doing!

We had a forklift truck given to us which was badly needed for the work but none of the usual team of men had a licence to drive it. We then discovered that one of the new volunteers who had been helping us for about a month had a licence to drive one. God's timing was again perfect. All of these men are past retiring age. But then, Moses was eighty years of age when the Lord called him!

The warehouse also seems to have played a significant part in the course of some becoming Christians. One day one of our faithful helpers came to our warehouse asking if he could bring two friends who were eager to help. They themselves were not Christians but their wives were and attended their local church. Alan was glad of the extra help and willingly agreed. What wonderful workers they were and when much later they offered to travel to Romania with the convoy Alan gladly accepted, especially as one of the men drove an articulated lorry. They were such an asset to the team and were to accompany us on many occasions. What a joy it was for the wives when a little while later they both became Christians. Was it the prayer meetings held each morning on the trips to Romania? Was it the various conversations with the brothers on the trip? Was it the witness of the lovely Christians in Romania or perhaps the church services that they attended whilst they were there? Probably it was a combination of all these things which led them to open up their hearts to the Holy Spirit of God.

We have many different things come into the warehouse that we cannot immediately place. One of these items was an almost new electric buggy. We had had it in for a little while and had been keeping it until we knew of a real need for it.

One day Alan picked up a Christian circular from the internet asking if anyone had an electric wheelchair for a severely handicapped boy called Ciprian who lived with his family who were extremely poor. Well, we didn't have an electric wheelchair but we did have this rather special buggy. We contacted the Christian young man whose name was on the circular and discovered that he was a Canadian doing missionary work in Romania, and had come across this family. Ciprian had a very old wheelchair but because his hands were not strong enough he was not able to turn the wheels and spent most of his time shuffling across the floor. We agreed that the electric buggy would be ideal for him and more than he could ever have dreamed of. We arranged to meet the Canadian and he would direct us to the house in the village. It was a hazardous journey over the mountains with deep snow but eventually Alan and the men, with the Canadian, reached the house.

How can we begin to describe the joy and wonderment on the faces of the whole family when they arrived with the special buggy? It took hardly any time for Ciprian to master which buttons to press so that he could travel back and fore.

After making sure that he was really in control of the buggy and understood how to operate it, the men prepared to leave. The father stepped forward. He was a deacon in the local church and said that he wanted to read from the Scriptures and pray before they left. He read from the book of Ruth where Ruth says to Naomi "Your God [is] my God," and then he said, "The same God that you worship in your country is the same God that we worship here in Romania, you are our brothers in Christ. This God has answered our prayers. We have been praying for two years for an electric wheelchair for Ciprian. As well as answering our prayers He has done more than we could have ever thought or imagined. To have an electric buggy like this was beyond our wildest dreams."

He then said, "Please let us now pray," and as they

were a Pentecostal family they all prayed together, including all the youngsters in the family. The men were moved to tears as they saw Ciprian, although he couldn't speak properly because of his handicap, making noises and obviously praying too as he lifted his hands to heaven and thanked God for His very special gift

It is amazing how many things have been packed in the warehouse by mistake. One of the men went to go home only to find that his anorak was nowhere to be seen. It had obviously been packed by mistake. He very graciously said he would manage with his other coat rather than try and find it amongst the dozens of packed boxes.   Another man went to use his mobile phone, only to discover that his coat had been packed with the mobile phone in it. We had to dial his mobile so that we could hear which box the ringing was coming from!

On another occasion I had been home and Alan came home from the warehouse disgusted. "Would you believe that anyone would send dirty underclothes?" he said. "There was a bag of clothes, the dresses and cardigans were like new so they were packed, but in amongst them were these soiled underclothes. I threw them straight in the bin - I just can't understand people." A few days later I went to do my mothers washing to find the black bag had disappeared. It had obviously got mixed with the others that were in the house and gone to the warehouse. Her dirty underclothes had been thrown out and the new dresses and cardigans that my sister and I had bought her about a month before were packed ready for Romania somewhere in the warehouse!

Incidentally, the boxes that we use only had to be

paid for on one occasion. We are very kindly given the "seconds" from a number of manufacturers, for which we are so grateful.

As I pack with others in the warehouse I believe that it is the Lord's work and that He ultimately is in charge of all that we do; He truly guides us, often without our realizing it, and that each box goes exactly where it should.

We have been shown that this is true in so many ways - let me share a few stories with you.

Just before going on one of our journeys, we sent out our needs list as usual, asking for many different things. We also asked for people to make up food boxes for poor families. Because people were so generous, we received six hundred food boxes. As we had so many, we decided to share them out and distribute them to the many different places that we support. So some went to Dr Vali and his wife Jeni working with street children, some went to Dr Florea working with children including Gypsy children, some went to our friends Carmen and Dorin who work with poor families in Ploiesti - and so on. We actually left parcels at about ten different places.

When we first met Carmen and Dorin they were living in very small rented accommodation. They had a tiny kitchen and two other small rooms, plus a toilet and washbasin. They lived there with their three children. Dorin, the father, slept on the kitchen floor because of the lack of space. Although they were not well off themselves they distributed fairly the things that we were able to take over for all the poor villages around them.

On one of our visits we heard that the government had found the previous owners of the house, and they wanted it back. It had been taken in Ceausescu's time and Carmen and Dorin would therefore be without a home. We were concerned about their situation and shared it with a few friends on our return. Together with them, we were able to buy a small house for Carmen and Dorin into which they joyfully moved. At last Dorin could sleep with his lovely wife! At last they could have a good hot bath! This young couple now work for a Canadian Christian charity which supports poor families in Romania financially. Together, they are making a real difference in people's lives.

When we returned on our next visit Carmen and Dorin asked us if we had time to visit a young lady who had received one of our boxes. She had a story she would like to share with us. Of course, we said that we would make time and so set off to visit Angelika.

On the way, Carmen explained that Angelika was a single mother and had had a little girl by a Turkish Cypriot. She had been a nightclub singer and had also been into other undesirable things which had earned her a lot of money and gold. However, she had been wonderfully saved and had then felt she could no longer keep what she had earned because it had been earned in the wrong way. So she had given it away and as a result was now living in a communal home with her little girl.

The communal home left a lot to be desired and the room that Angelika and her daughter had been given was very small. We were delighted however, to see a Bible open on the table, and she was clearly overjoyed to greet us. She explained to us through Carmen that she had received one of our food boxes. She had been so delighted when she opened it because inside were many things that she needed.

The person who had packed the box had put a card on the top on which was her name and address. Now people do not normally do this, (they just pack their box and that's it.) Angelika was so grateful for her box that she decided that she would write to this lady and thank her, which she did, telling her a little about herself. The lady wrote back,

Thank you so much for writing to me, and telling me about yourself. I want you to know what a tremendous blessing that was for me. As I packed the box, as I put in each item, I said to the Lord, "Lord, will You please make sure that my box reaches a single mother."

This lady had been a single mother herself at one time and knew how difficult it was. That was why she had made this request. Out of the six hundred boxes taken and deposited all over the country the Lord had made sure that her box had reached a single mother!

When Alan and I talked about it afterwards we said that even when those boxes were being loaded God had had to make sure that that box was loaded on the right place on the lorry, so that it did not come off at Dr Vali's or Doctor Florea's or any of the other places. It had to be loaded so that it came off at Carmen and Dorin's.

That was remarkable enough. But then, as Alan pointed out, He had to make sure that Carmen picked up the right box as well. What a wonderful God we have! We know that He is mighty and powerful. We accept readily that He created the world and us because He is God. The wonder to us is that He is in the small things and that He is concerned about every detail of our lives. What a joy to belong to One such as this!

A little later, I came across a verse in Proverbs

that I had not noticed before. It said,

We can make our plans, but the final outcome is in God's hands.

Proverbs 16:1. *The Living Bible.*

Well, we pack the boxes and the Lord decides where they should go. He even decides where birthday cakes go as the following story illustrates.

A bakery has been generous to us over many years, giving us pallets of cakes to take over to Romania. Apparently they are either 'seconds' or returns but invariably we have got a job to spot why they are 'seconds'. Before one of our journeys we were given a large number of really lovely birthday cakes and, because there were so many, we divided them up between various places.

We left some with Carmen and Dorin where we had left the food boxes previously, together with parcels of clothes, medicines, shoes and other things for poor families. We had a letter from Carmen when we returned home telling us this story.

We were quite busy with other things for a few days and decided that we would go to the various families in the village the following week. However, the next day I said to Dorin that I felt I should go to visit a particular family with the things that they needed, and that I should go on that very day. I was happy to leave the other families until the following week. I gathered their things together and, really as an afterthought, put one of your lovely birthday cakes complete with fancy packaging on the top.

When I arrived at the house the family was there. I delivered the other things, then took in the cake. As she saw the cake the mother wept tears as her little boy took it and ran to show the rest of the family. It was his birthday that day! He had asked his mother days before if she would make him a cake for his birthday. Sadly she told him that she couldn't afford to buy the ingredients to make him one.

Now to him had been delivered his very own extra special birthday cake!

Why did Carmen decide that day to go to that particular family and why did she decide to take a birthday cake?

Our dear, loving, heavenly Father wanted that little boy to have a birthday cake. He was at work yet again. Carmen had so obviously been guided by the Holy Spirit.

What an encouragement for all of us who work at the warehouse and also for all of those who loyally support us in giving us things to take out! They *will* go to exactly the right place. The Lord is in charge.

Another time we were given a brand new dressmakers dummy - still in its box. "What am I going to do with this?" I pondered and put it to one side. When the packing had been finished, I again looked at the dummy. I knew many ladies in Romania who did sewing. They had been sewing for many years and were quite adept at making things for themselves without a dummy. Would any of these ladies need or even use one? I went through the names of about a dozen ladies and still did not have any inspiration. In the end, out of sheer desperation, I thought that I would give it to one of those ladies and that she could maybe pass it on if it was not suitable. So I marked her name on the box and off it went to Romania.

We were staying with this particular family in Romania for a few days and working out from there. We arrived quite late at night and unloaded many things there - parcels to be delivered by them, things for their church, clothes for them to distribute to poor people and, of course, the dummy in the box. We then went to bed.

We were out early in the morning to deliver at the local orphanage and did not return until late at night. When we did, the lady of the house threw her arms around me and cried, thanking me for her special gift. What special gift? I couldn't remember bringing her a special gift as such.

She then explained that she worked (as I knew) in a department store selling shoes. There was one section where they sold clothes and they had one dummy to display the clothes. The dummy was broken and rather scruffy. Two and a half years ago she had mentioned to the lady in charge of the department that if ever she was going to throw it out would she please give it to her first. She said that she had always found difficulty in making clothes for herself and she thought that it would help her.

Two weeks before we came she had been trying to pin on a skirt that she was making for herself and said to her daughter, "I don't think that my dream will ever come true. That dummy is still in the shop and I don't think that they will ever get rid of it."

We then arrived, not with a broken, grubby dummy, but with a brand new expanding and contracting dressmaker's dummy, complete in its box.

She wept tears of joy as she said to me, "I'm crying to realize that God loves me so much to send me this. I would not have prayed for it - it is not a 'need'. It was just a dream that was in my heart. Nobody knew - but God did, and He chose to show His love to me in this way."

Yes, my dear sister, God knew your heart and He knows your struggles and your difficulties. He also knows how much you love Him - it was His love gift to you.

Thank You Lord, that when I am uncertain about where things should go, You guide.

The same lady received another "love gift" from the Lord many years later.

It was just before Christmas and we received a letter from her asking if by any chance we had a record player in the warehouse. She explained that the old record player we had taken over for her a long time ago with some Christian records that we had been given had finally broken. She was just wondering if we had another old one in the warehouse and, if it was not allocated for elsewhere, could she possibly have it? She said, "It means so much to me to be able to play carols on it at Christmas time but, of course, it's not a need so I will understand if it's not possible."

We looked in the warehouse and sadly we did not have one. It was only a couple of days before we were leaving so there was now no chance of getting one in. We had sent out our needs list a long time ago and had had our receiving-in days. So that, unfortunately, was that.

The day before leaving, Alan and the men had loaded the final lorry on the Monday. They stood talking outside the warehouse for a little while.

Alan said, "I don't suppose any of you have got a record player that you don't want, have you?"

"That's amazing that you should ask that," said one of the men. "I have one." When Alan asked where it was he said, "I've actually got one in the back of my car over there. A lady brought it to church last night. I didn't know whether you needed record players or not. Anyway, I put it in the boot of my car last night and was going to ask you today, but we had been so busy that I forgot."

Alan went to get the record player from his car – it was brand new, still in the polystyrene packaging!

Dear Salomica was able to play her carols at Christmas after all!

CHAPTER 6

Travelling Through Romania

Support for Romania is totally a voluntary work; nobody gets paid.

We hire the trucks from a national firm that has been very good to us over the years, although we do now have three of our very own. One of the trucks came to us by an amazing way.

We heard that another charity had hired a truck and it had broken down in Austria. The hire firm did not want to go to the expense of going out there and putting it right and then bringing it home. The charity that hired it did not want to do this either. So the hire firm said that anyone who was prepared to go out and repair it and bring it home could have it! We heard about this, so one New Year's Eve, Alan and three men went out and repaired the truck and brought it home triumphantly. That was in 1998 and by May 2007 it had done over fifty journeys.

We drive convoys of trucks and normally there are two drivers per truck. It is hard, concentrated driving. Crossing borders was never easy and required a lot of patience and tenacity. We have all had to grow in that area over the years, and that has not always been easy either. The customs officials made it very difficult and although our papers were always correct, they seemed to delight in being plain awkward in various ways.

I remember on one particular occasion standing for ages in one queue with some papers while Alan queued in another. When it was my turn the man behind the window put up his hand to indicate for me to wait and then proceeded slowly, very slowly, to eat a bar of chocolate, bit by bit, with his feet on the desk, then finishing it and slowly, again very slowly, folding the paper and putting it in the bin. I honestly could have hit him. (Sorry, Lord!!) What an absolute disgrace!

The convoys of lorries are always full to capacity. Among the supplies are often about six hundred parcels for about two hundred poor families in Romania. These families have been adopted by Christian families in and around Cardiff who twice a year send parcels. We have one whole day and one evening especially designated for people to bring these to the warehouse. There they are coded and placed in the appropriate place. A card is filed for each person with the sender's name on one side and the recipient's name on the other, together with the number of parcels being sent. This system has worked well over the years.

On arriving in Romania those parcels we cannot deliver ourselves because of time are left at certain points with a Christian brother or sister, who will either deliver them personally or telephone the families to collect them. Others they will send by rail or post and they all get there.

Our friend Sammy* in Suceava deals with many of them. However, we could not leave them with him until we were leaving his apartment (where we stayed) as we and others were sleeping in the rooms.

---

* Sadly, Sammy died in January 2007 but his widow Salomica is carrying on the work.

So on the day we were leaving we had to carry the parcels to the fourth floor, which was quite a task. We do ask that the parcels be a reasonable size but people get carried away. We try to tell them gently that many of the parcels have to be delivered to fourth- or fifth-floor apartment blocks where there are no lifts.

It takes us three days to get to Romania, and that is with very hard driving. We eat and drink as we travel, but stop at small hotels along the way. We are then in Romania for about ten days delivering and unloading at the various places. We usually work from about 8.30am until about 10.00pm (if everything goes smoothly). Occasionally we make shorter trips.

When drivers express an interest in helping us by driving to Romania we explain that each person has to pay his own expenses, including the ferry crossing and the two overnight stops in a hotel. We have found over the years that people are willing to do this gladly. In this way nothing is taken out of the charity. Drivers come with us from all walks of life, mainly Christians although we have taken drivers who are not, but who are sympathetic to the work. We stress to new volunteers that they have to be adaptable. They always say they are, but sometimes they do not reckon on how adaptable they have to be!

They might have to sleep in strange places, according to where they are staying. I have slept under a kitchen table, on a concrete slab halfway up a wall (I felt as though I was in a morgue) and had to share a double bed with another man as well as Alan. Fortunately he was a dear friend of ours, and a deacon in another church (that made it

53

respectable, didn't it?), but the dear family gave us all that they had, and slept themselves on the kitchen floor. How could we refuse to sleep there when so much love had been shown?

Another problem can be the water supply. Either it is cold or non-existent. I remember one man complaining, "I'm used to a hot shower every morning." To which Alan replied, "This is where you have to be adaptable." The discomfort applies not only to washing. Sometimes the toilet is an outside loo, with, of course, no flushing facilities, plus the proverbial newspaper cut up, hanging on a hook with string.

The food sometimes, especially out in the countryside, can be a little unpalatable. It is rather hard to look as if you are enjoying chicken that has not been properly cooked, with chips that are also half-cooked, and chicken fat poured over both. This is particularly so when the meal is breakfast and the time is 6.30 a.m. Another breakfast delicacy to which we are not accustomed is boiled nettles. As we eat we have a little prayer that we say, "Lord we will get it down if you will help us to keep it down!" There are, however, special families that we stay with in Romania. Not only are the ladies of the houses excellent cooks and the resulting meals wonderful, but they and their families have proved to be very dear friends.

I must mention, however, three homes in particular where we are given a royal welcome. One is in Oradea where Victoria is an excellent cook. We are very spoiled with superb food there, as is also the case in Cluj and Suceava where Nora and Salomica look after us equally well. These three homes are very special to us, as are the families that live there.

We do now have a core of experienced drivers whom we use regularly, and by now they are able to cope with all kinds of situations.

It is very important to keep together in convoy, otherwise there is every possibility of getting lost, and if one of the lorries breaks down, at least we are all together. For my part, one thing I do insist on now is that I drive behind Alan's lorry (which is always the leader) and I make sure that I keep up with him, and that when we change drivers, my co-driver does as well. I have every reason to do this because over the years I have had my share of mishaps.

There is now a by-pass around Budapest in Hungary - thankfully. However, before the by-pass we had to drive right through the centre of Budapest - which was a nightmare. It is such a busy city, with traffic coming from all directions. On one occasion I had been held up at the traffic lights and Alan, mistakenly thinking I was behind him, had gone on. I thought the way was straight ahead, but he had turned right and I quickly recognized that I had gone the wrong way. The trouble was, the rest of the convoy had followed me. I didn't have a clue how to proceed; the volume of traffic was tremendous with drivers impatiently blasting their horns as I dithered. I knew I would have to get back to where I went wrong but that was easier said than done. I decided to go for it down a particular direction and at least try. I was so scared; it was like being in Piccadilly Circus in the rush-hour. The other trucks dutifully and bravely were trying to keep up behind. After about ten minutes I suddenly spotted Alan's lorry on another road. He had come looking for us and was waving frantically for me to get over to where he was and to follow him. With a great struggle I managed to do this, and together with the other trucks, got in behind him. I felt a nervous wreck and yet was so relieved to have found him. When we reached a quieter road Alan signalled me to pull in which we all did.

I jumped out of the truck. "I'm so relieved to have found you," I cried. "Oh, Alan I'm so sorry. I went the wrong way and I didn't know how to get back. Thank you for finding me. I was so scared."

Alan glared at me. "You're stupid, utterly stupid! How could you make that mistake, taking all the trucks with you?"

I had been so glad and relieved to see him; now I was angry. "Don't call me stupid. I'm not stupid, you should have made sure that I was behind you. That's the trouble; you don't care; you don't watch out for me; I'm just one of the men as far as you're concerned. I've a good mind to just leave this lorry here and go home, but as I can't do that - I'm never coming to Romania again. That's it!"

I stalked back to the lorry, where my co-driver sheepishly asked, "Is everything all right?"

"Fine," I said through gritted teeth, "no problem."

Of course, as soon as we had the opportunity we apologized to each other. Alan had been so concerned over losing the convoy, and for me also that he said things in anger and I was so thankful that we had found him that I too acted badly. Oh, the joys of working together! I think that emotions run very high anyway on these journeys and, coupled with tiredness, can have a strange effect on one's character.

There was another time when I lost Alan, which was to have much more serious consequences. I and another driver were driving behind him in Austria with a van and trailer, when a police car pulled up alongside us and indicated for us to pull over at the service station which was coming up. We did this believing that the lorry in front had seen this happen and would wait for us.

The police then indicated that we had a faulty red light on the trailer and that this needed to be mended. They then left us to sort it out. The driver said that he knew what it was (some sort of loose connection) and was able to put it right within minutes so that we were able to get back on the road. We were rather disturbed not to find the other lorry as we travelled on and then after an hours travelling, we suddenly realized that we were heading back the way that we had come originally. We had gone in the wrong direction when we left the service station! We now had to get back on the right road. This was going to be no mean feat and neither I nor the driver was that good on directions. However, after about another hour we managed it and set off confidently, understanding that by now Alan had probably not seen us go off and had gone on to our destination not knowing what else to do. It was now one o'clock in the morning and we settled down for what we knew would be a good three-and-a-half hour drive. The roads were really quiet at this time in the morning and we felt that it would be a straightforward run. The other driver had completed his hours of driving and I was due to take over. We had seen a lay-by sign and had decided to pull in there and change over.

All of a sudden, there was a terrific crash, and I found myself going round and round in circles within a bright light. I was completely disorientated and thought that I was coming out of some sort of anaesthetic. I came to, aware that I was now in the back of the van.

The van and trailer had been hit in the rear by an articulated lorry that had gone out of control because the driver had fallen asleep. The lorry had hit the van knocking it over to the other side of the road, where both the van and the trailer had overturned and then sprung upright again. The trailer, we could see, was a complete write-off and the van very badly damaged. The road was strewn with pieces of china (we had mugs, plates and honey in the trailer which we were bringing back to sell), clothing, passports and other documents. By now other people had arrived and the police had to divert the traffic.

We both climbed out of the van hardly daring to believe that we were alive and literally shaking from head to toe. I guess it was the shock of it all and we stood there surrounded by people who spoke no English.

I managed to explain to the police that I needed to telephone my husband. I realized that by now Alan would have been at the hotel where we were due to stay the night, anxiously waiting for us. With help from the onlookers, the van and trailer were pushed into the lay-by that we were making for, and my co-driver stayed in the van with one of the policemen, while I accompanied the other policeman to the police station. He shot off at a terrific speed. I was still shaking from the accident and felt that I was going to break into tears. I also knew that I had no idea as to the name of the hotel or the number - I just could not remember. How on earth I was going to ring Alan who was our lifeline. I prayed silently, "Lord please, please help me. I'm so scared and so desperate, what am I going to do?"

We arrived at the police station. I spoke no German and the policeman spoke no English and we just looked at each other.

Then the Lord took over. How I praised His name! He reminded me that a brother who had been to Romania with us before would have the name and number of the hotel. He reminded me of the brother's telephone number and to this day (I cannot remember how) He enabled me to explain to the policeman that I needed to ring the UK and then a Cardiff number.

I got through to Ron who was awakened from his sleep - it was still the early hours of the morning. I explained why I was ringing and asked for the number of the hotel. I then rang the hotel in Germany and Alan was called to the telephone. He had been desperately worried and was so relieved to hear my voice. He was concerned that we were both alright and I was able to tell him where we were and exactly where he would find us. It was going to take him over three hours to return to us.

The policeman then dropped me back to the other driver, took his mate with him, and we were left in the van to await Alan and the other driver.

We put blankets around ourselves. We were so cold in the lay-by and talked about how the Lord had truly protected us. We both felt that we had had a little bit of whiplash, but were amazed that we had come out of the crash alive. I knew personally too, that He had undertaken for me in a remarkable way. I was about to fall apart but He took control and gave me such a calmness that I was able to know exactly what to do. We truly believe that the prayers of God's people are so important while we are away and we knew that many people always pray for our protection. So, please carry on praying!

When Alan eventually arrived with his co-driver and saw the state of the vehicles he could not believe it. "I didn't realize it was this bad," he said, "you were so calm." "Thank You, Lord," I murmured. The four of us put our arms around each other as we stood in the lay-by and thanked Him from the bottom of our hearts for looking after us.

Now we had to decide what to do. It was obvious that we could not do anything with the vehicles, and that a garage would have to tow them away. The trailer was indeed a write-off and we wondered whether the van was too, but thought that just maybe it could somehow be put right.

Alan went off to find a garage and came back saying that they would come in a couple of hours, so in the meantime we would need to empty the van and collect the few bits that were left in the trailer as the four of us would need to travel home in one lorry, leaving the van there.

We opened the back door of the van and what a sight met our eyes. We were bringing back large churns of honey from a Christian beekeeper putting it into jars and selling it for him. He then used the money to buy materials for a church that he and some other Christians were building in their village. The churns had fallen over in the crash, the lids had come off, and everything in the van, including our personal belongings, was covered in honey. We spent the next couple of hours trying to clear the things up so that we could transfer them to the lorry. However, we had only cold water and some rags. We did not succeed very well.

From then on I made sure that I stuck to Alan like glue (not honey!).

I remember a time when Alan and I had travelled

alone to Romania in a lorry and had reached the Hungarian/Romanian border, to be asked, "Are you thinking of going into Romania with that lorry?" Rather a surly question but, yes, we were.

"Well, there is no diesel in Romania," the guards smirked, "it has all been reclaimed by the government for agricultural purposes – there is none in the pumps, so you'll have to turn back."

We were not sure if they were telling the truth; the Hungarians are not particularly fond of the Romanians and often resent aid going in.

We decided to go in and see what was what anyway. The trouble was, as we approached the first petrol station we realized that they were probably telling the truth. The nozzle was placed over the pump, which always meant no fuel. When we enquired of the attendant if that was so, he confirmed what the border guards had told us, that all the diesel had been reclaimed from the pumps by the government.

We sat and looked at each other. What on earth were we going to do?

"Well, we can't turn back now we have come this far," Alan said. "There are people relying on this aid."

"So, we will go in knowing there is no diesel in the pumps," I returned, "and what's going to happen then."

We looked at each other and decided between us that there and then we would pray asking the Lord somehow to get us where we needed to go (we were going over a thousand miles all around the country). We prayed what to us seemed an impossible prayer, "Lord, please somehow supply the diesel to get this lorry – your lorry - where it needs to go" – and off we went.

The first time we saw the needle approaching the red we felt a bit shaky, but said quietly, "Lord, please, we are trusting You," and continued to drive to our first destination.

We delivered our parcels to a Christian brother who joyfully received them and then asked, "How are you managing for diesel, as there is none in the country? I have a small tank in my back garden if you would like a couple of gallons," he added. We gave thanks and continued on our journey, each time the needle got towards the red the Lord supplied the diesel. We had half a bucket from a brother on top of a mountain, some from a tractor, and so on. We were able to complete our itinerary all over Romania on diesel supplied by the Lord. What a wonderful journey that was as we saw right before our very eyes the Lord at work in a miraculous way!

Is it because they have to trust God for their many needs that the Christians in Romania have such a strong faith? We miss out in so many ways because things are so much easier for us here. Over the years I have learned that the Romanian people have so much to teach us.

Hotel accommodation is a long way from matching that of the Hilton or the Marriot. On one occasion we were travelling over the Carpathian Mountains in very bad weather. It was horrendous, with so much snow and ice. The lorries had slipped and slithered and now one had finally broken down. A little way ahead we spotted what I suppose could be described as a small hotel and decided that the only thing to do was to stay there for the night. It was late, and we would perhaps be better able to sort things out in the morning.

The rooms left a lot to be desired, with no carpet on the floor, broken curtains and bedclothes that were far from clean. However, we were so exhausted that we fell in to bed and slept soundly. The next morning I was covered in red bites which itched badly and I realized that I had had company in my bed in the night – not only Alan but fleas!!

We did not bother to stop for breakfast; we couldn't have coped with food poisoning as well. We only visit Romania for a couple of weeks and then we can come back to our comfortable homes. I would find it so hard to live there.

Carmen and Darius live in a town called Deva. Her father lives over the mountains in Moldavia, a province of Romania, not to be confused with Moldova, which borders Romania. We frequently transport sacks of potatoes from him to his daughter. He lives in the countryside so he grows his own. We laugh and think it's all part of the service and we are delighted to be able to help this couple in a small way.

One night Alan and I had the potatoes on board and were aiming for Deva where we were going to sleep. We would deliver the potatoes the following morning with all the other things that we had for the young couple to distribute. The family knew that we were coming - we often slept there. However we had been held up and were well behind schedule and did not arrive until 1.30 in the morning.

We wearily got our overnight bag out of the lorry and climbed the two floors of the apartment block and rang the bell. No answer. We tried again - still no answer. They had probably given up on us - we had been due to arrive at ten o'clock.

We didn't like to go on ringing at that time, so we

decided that we would have to sleep in the cab of the lorry. The trouble was it was winter and absolutely freezing.

We settled down in the cab. I just could not sleep, I was frozen. Alan was fitfully dozing, but I have never been so cold in all my life. I did not want to worry him because I knew that there was nothing he could do, but I thought to myself, I really think I am going to get hypothermia. We had been in the lorry two hours by now - I could have cried. Suddenly Alan shot up, "It's no good, we can't stay here," then looking at my pinched face, or what he could see of it, "we will have to go in the apartment block and sleep in the hallway. At least it will be a bit warmer." He could hardly hold the keys to lock the lorry door as we stumbled into the apartment block. "I think we'll try the door once more," he said. So up we went.

The family heard and came to the door in their nightclothes. I was shaking from head to foot by now. They took one look at us and said, "Get in our bed immediately." We did, as our friends took themselves off into the living-room. Never has a bed been so welcome. It had been minus twenty when we were in the lorry. They had thought that we had been held up and were not coming.

"Don't you ever do that again," they said. "You ring and ring until we answer."

Of course, then we did not have a mobile phone. We do now and have found it so helpful at such times.

When a tiler was needed for the church at Chisineu-Cris, an experienced tiler we know kindly agreed to do the job. So Alan and I took him over by car. We stopped the first night at an Etap Hotel. We knew that we were going to be late so Alan telephoned ahead. The hotel operated one of those systems whereby you give them your credit card number and they then give you the code for the front gate and your room number. These numbers have to be punched into a panel outside the room that you have been given in order for the door to open. We have used the Etap hotels many times and this system works very well, as often at ten o'clock or later in the night, no one is on duty.

We duly arrived and went to our respective rooms. It was very late at night. Alan punched our number in but it did not work. He tried again and as the numbers rattled in we heard a noise inside the room, and a man's voice shouting. Alan shouted through the door, "We are trying to get in, this is our room." Back came the man's angry voice, "This is *our* room. You obviously have got the wrong number. Will you please go away, we are trying to sleep." It was now nearly one o'clock in the morning.

We looked at each other. "This is definitely the number that I was given," said Alan. "You know what has happened, they've double-booked the room. There is a coin-box telephone downstairs. We'll go down and see if there is an emergency number that we can contact."

Of course, the information by the telephone was not in English and there did not appear to be any number to ring.

"What on earth are we going to do?" I said to Alan. "All I can think of is going out to sleep in the car but it will be freezing out there."

"Or . . .?" Alan said grinning.

I read his thoughts. "Oh, no, Alan we can't. We don't know Colin (the tiler) very well. How can we knock him up and tell him that we've got to share his bedroom."

"Well," Alan said matter-of-factly, "It'll be alright, I'll share the double bed with him and you can climb up to the single bunk above the bed."

"Lord, what shall we do?" we said together. Just then a man came into the hotel and he could obviously see that we had a problem. However, he spoke very little English and we found it rather difficult to explain. He eventually understood, "Last night I stay in room here," he said. "Tonight different room, but . . ." And he pulled a piece of paper from his pocket with a code number on. Then he said, "This was number of my room last night, maybe tonight it is free."

We went upstairs together and punched in the code, the door opened and the room was empty. We turned to thank the man but he had gone. "I wonder," I said to Alan, "if that man was an angel sent by God to help us." Next day the receptionist was so apologetic, they had double-booked the room causing us the problem.

Thank You, Lord, for taking pity on us and on Colin!

I remember on one journey how we had had a very difficult time before we finally reached our small hotel to sleep for the night. It was very late and we had not been able to reach the hotel that we had booked so we went to another one just hoping that we would get in. There were seven of us, five men, Alan and myself. The owner took us to a room saying, "I'm sorry this is all I can manage. If you can make it do, you are welcome to it."

There were five beds. I could not believe my eyes as one of our company who was obviously more exhausted than the rest of us exclaimed, "At last a bed!" took off his trousers in front of me, and stood poised in his underpants before diving into bed. This brother would have had a fit if I had told him the next day what he had done. He would have been mortified. He was an upright and very private man and obviously very, very tired!

We ended up with Alan sharing a bed with one of the men and me sleeping on the floor.

CHAPTER 7

Beloved Physicians

Dr Vali and his wife Jeni look after up to 150 street children in a converted cinema in Otelu Rosu. They also have babies to care for. He is not only giving these children and teenagers a home, but a Christian upbringing and an education as well. Many of the older young people have become Christians and help in the home with the cooking and the cultivation of vegetables. They have a piece of land at the rear of the building in which they grow things. We have taken over gardening tools and vegetable seeds to help them, among many other things. They also have a cow which is milked each day, and a small bakery installed by another charity in which they bake not only their own bread but bread for the local village as well. We took over a large dough mixer which we were given.

Dr Vali is well respected in Romania and the state has grudgingly had to admit that he is doing an excellent job, so much so that when they could no longer run the state orphanage next door to his they asked him if he would be prepared to take it on. When he told us this we said to him, "Vali, how could you cope? There are over three hundred children there, surely it is impossible." He looked at us, smiling gently, "I'm signing the papers on Monday. I must do it."

So, he took on the orphanage with all the responsibility that that brings. He truly would have to rely on the Lord to help him in every possible way.

Ceausescu's palace

This is the palace that Ceausescu's wife had built for herself

A common village scene. An elderly lady washes her clothes in the stream, accompanied by ducks and a pig.

Peter and Rodica who run a christian foundation in Cluj helping needy people. We take many things over for them.

Some of the incontinence pads that we delivered.

People waiting inside the Foundation for medicines, food, incontinence pads, clothes etc.

This is the moment when we realised we needed a larger warehouse!

The team of ladies taking a break from packing to have their photograph taken.

The men stop for a break.

Our Talbot Green warehouse - 12,000 square feet in size - loaned to us free of charge.

Arthur and Paul make sure all our bicycles are in good working order before being dispatched to Romania.

A pastor receives his bicycle.

Ciprian sits in his new wheelchair.

Carmen and Dorin, our faithful Romanian helpers from Ploiesti.

One of our convoy of lorries

The truck that was rescued from Austria. By April 2007 it had completed more than fifty trips to Romania.

Our Romanian friend Sami, who helped us with the delivery of many parcels. Sadly he died in January 2007.

A family receives boxes sent by their sponsor.

Delivering a Combine Harvester to Romania. The tractor unit and low loader to transport it were loaned to us free of charge.

Christmas Shoe Boxes from one of the schools that have supported us
for many years.

We were speaking at this school assembly. They also support us with
Christmas Shoe Boxes.

Some of the pupils helping us to load.

The badly damaged van and trailer after our serious accident.

Colin preparing to tile the floor of the church hall at Chisineu Cris.
He also laid the carpet in the church.

On the next visit we made to him he showed us around the place. He had already with some of the older street children, painted it right the way through. As we passed through the utility area, we saw two large commercial washing machines. "Well, at least you have got these two good washing machines," Alan remarked.

"We have now," said Vali, "but the state has said it wants them back, so I will not have them in a few weeks time."

"How will you manage," I gasped, "with washing for all these children?"

"Ann, it is the Lord's work and He will somehow provide them," he said with a smile.

We knew that the type of washing machine he needed would cost a thousand pounds each, and we did not have that money. Where would it come from?

We had been back home about a week and Alan was looking in his personal telephone directory for the name of a man that he had forgotten beginning with W. As he flicked through the W's he saw Washing Machines Commercial and a telephone number. He remembered that many years ago we had been given this number but had never rung it. He thought to himself, "It would be interesting to see if they have got any washing machines there. I know we have not got any money to buy them, but I could just ask."

He dialled the number and asked the man if he had any large, reconditioned commercial washing machines there. "It's funny you should ring," said the man, "I had two in from a hospital yesterday. They've just gone on to a new type of machine and they are in excellent condition."

"How much are they?" Alan asked.

"A thousand pounds each," the man replied.

Alan came downstairs and told me all this and then said, "You'll never guess what I've done."

I looked at him. "You haven't said that we will have them, have you?"

Alan looked rather sheepish. "Yes."

"But Alan, we haven't got the money. How are we going to pay for them?"

Alan took hold of my hands. "Ann, Dr Vali has got to have those washing machines. I believe that I was meant to order them in faith - trust me."

I did, and I do, trust Alan. I always think that he has his head in the clouds but his feet on the ground - he is not one to do something like that lightly.

My trust in Alan was not misplaced, neither was his trust in the Lord.

Two days later we had an anonymous gift put through the door of three thousand pounds to be used in whatever way we thought fit. It was enough not only to pay for the washing machines but more than enough to pay for the cost of transporting them. Alan and I were the only two people who knew about Dr Vali's need for the washing machines. Oh, I forgot, most importantly there was one other person, the Lord!

Dr Vali has since opened a number of centres where he feeds poor people each day, and the Lord is continuing to supply his needs.

We are told that there are as many street children in Romania now than there were before the revolution. Many have run away from orphanages where they have been badly treated. Even more sadly, many have been put on the streets by their parents who cannot afford to keep them and felt they would have a better chance of surviving on the streets. We have actually been at the traffic lights at two o'clock in the morning when two little ones no more than three years old have climbed up on the lorry steps asking for 'pîine' (bread). At that particular time it was pouring with rain and they were absolutely soaked. It really was heartbreaking. Adi's story is particularly moving.

Adi came from a very poor Gypsy family. His mother had already sold his sister and was offering Adi for sale as well. One dreads to think what these dear children were to be used for. However, when the man who wanted to buy Adi came to see him, he refused to buy him saying he wasn't worth anything. This was because he was in very poor health and extremely malnourished. In desperation his mother put him on the streets to beg, cutting his tongue first of all so that more people would be sympathetic towards him in the hope that he would be able to bring in more money. Some time later his mother died and sadly his father ceased to care for his son. But somebody had seen Adi begging on the streets and it was obvious he was very ill so he was admitted to hospital. Dr Vali was told about him and with Jeni and a helper called Nuti, they visited Adi. Jeni and Nuti immediately wanted to take him back to the orphanage but Dr Vali was very reluctant to do this saying, "He will live no more than four weeks, and I don't want the responsibility of his death on my hands." However, Jeni and Nuti pleaded with him saying, "We will look after him and we believe we can save him." Dr Vali eventually gave in. Today Adi is a fine young man who is in Bible College and training to be an evangelist. He wants to go back to his Gypsy village to preach the gospel. Maybe he did not seem "worth anything" to the man who wanted to buy him, but he was worth much to a God who has transformed his life.

Dr Vali's children are surrounded with so much love, and these street children are different, they are caring, warm, polite and loving. Their lives have been transformed and many of them have become real Christians. On one visit I had to go downstairs in the cinema to fetch something and I was so moved to see about a dozen children between five and eight years old on their own singing "Jesus is Lord." They just smiled at me and carried on singing.

What wonderful work is going on in Otelu Rosu. Dr Vali once said to me, "Ann, I think when God called me to this work He put His hands over my eyes and did not take them off until I was in the middle of the work and there was no turning back. If I had known what He was going to ask me to do I would have turned and run."

There is a gentleman in Cardiff who has been giving us money to take out for Dr Vali for a good while. He has been extremely generous and has been giving us a thousand pounds every month. Dr Vali has been so grateful for this wonderful support.

At the beginning of one year we had a letter from Dr Vali asking us if this man would be able to send a year's money in advance. He could not pay the wages of those working with the street children and had other debts that he had to clear.

Alan and I looked at each other; there was no way we could ask this man for the money for the whole year. It would not be right. It would be an imposition. It might well be that he was not going to support Dr Vali this particular year anyway. We recognized Dr Vali's desperate need, but we just knew that there was no way we could do this. We were sad that we could not help in this way and after discussing it said that we would write to him and explain our feelings. We had not sent the letter when out of the blue one day we received a phone call from the brother who usually gave the money. "Alan," he said, "I hope it won't inconvenience you but there is going to be a change in my giving this year." Alan thought, "Well, it's as I thought, he's now going to have to stop his generous support." Alan listened in growing amazement as he said, "If it's all right with you, I would like to give my gift for Dr Vali in one lump sum. I have arranged to pay you a year in advance and the cheque for twelve thousand pounds is on its way!"

Alan was totally shocked, and came down from the office to tell me. Our friend had no idea, of course, of Dr Vali's need, but the Lord did and prompted him to decide to give us the annual gift to take over.

I know we should not be amazed at how God works but how can we help it? No wonder it is a delight to know and serve Him, He is so real.

Vali and Jeni, we admire you so much for dedicating your lives to this work, we are glad to be just a small part of it. "God is truly in this place."

Tim and Debbie are a young couple whom we have known for many years. Tim was a member of the young people's group that I and another friend ran. We were delighted when he came to the Lord and equally delighted to watch his strong Christian progress over many years. Tim eventually met and married Debbie and we were delighted to share in their wedding day.

Tim's mother and father live in Cardiff, so when Tim and Debbie came to visit them, they would also call and see us. It was always good to hear how they were doing and on one of their later visits they shared with us that although they had been married for thirteen years, sadly they had finally come to terms with the fact that they would not be able to have a family of their own. However, they had been passed for adoption and intended adopting, starting with a young baby and then adding to their family. We were thrilled to hear their news and delighted that at last it would seem they would have the family they so much desired. Over the years, Tim and Debbie had generously supported Dr Vali's work with the street children and we often took out gifts from them.

A short while after they had told us of their adoption plans, we had a telephone call from them saying that they had a holiday coming up and they thought it would be rather nice to visit Dr Vali and the street children. Could we arrange it for them? Well, we could, and we did, and Tim and Debbie flew out to visit Dr Vali.

While they were there the Lord spoke to them telling them that this was where he now wanted them to work, looking after the street children and helping Dr Vali. So in 2001 Tim and Debbie left the U.K. and bought themselves a house not far from the orphanage. They also (with their own money) bought another house and opened it as a baby orphanage where abandoned babies are taken. They have called this orphanage "Cristian" and have looked after many babies.

What happened to their adoption plans?

Happily, they are fostering twins who were abandoned, with a view to adopting them in the near future. They have left behind their comfortable lifestyle in obedience to God. It has not been easy for them and at the time of writing Tim has had to return to the U.K. to work for a period as a supply teacher in order to pay the wages of the people working in "Cristian".

What a dedicated couple they are! And now they are being supported not only by their home church but also by others who have heard of their work and send out financial aid through our charity.

Just before leaving on one of our journeys we had a letter from Tim and Debbie saying that they were sorry that they were late in sending in their request but some of the babies had developed bronchial problems. They had the medication in Romania but could not get children's face masks, which they badly needed to administer the treatment. Could we help? We did not really know what the asked-for face masks were like and could not possibly see our way clear to finding any before we went. All our medicine had been packed and even if somebody had packed face masks how would we find the box?

We decided that when we went to the warehouse on the Monday we would ask people there if they knew what they were like and maybe where we could try and get them. Alan and I usually go up earlier to the warehouse before the others arrive, to set things out. We had just opened the door when a car pulled up and we recognized the lady as one of our supporters.

"I know that you have had your receiving-in days, and you are packed and ready to go," she said. "I have had these things for a while now. I feel bad that I haven't brought them before but could you take them off my hands?"

Alan and I looked at each other and sighed. We did not really want any more things in the warehouse at this late stage. "How much have you got?" Alan asked.

"A full boot," she replied, "and it's a bit of a mixture really." We liked the lady very much, and she was not usually late in delivering things.

"Okay," said Alan, "We are busy - would you mind bringing the things in and putting them on the back table?" She was happy to do this and then left.

About half an hour later Alan was passing the table and said to me, "Look at that, there's a box marked "Adult Face Masks."

"So there is," I replied. "What a shame it's not for children."

"Well, we could open the box and see what they look like," Alan said, "and then at least we would know what we're looking for."

So between us we opened the box. Inside were dozens of face masks, but although the box had been marked "adults" they were children's face masks. We looked at each other absolutely astounded. If these face masks had come in at the "right" time they would have been packed in one of the many medical boxes and we doubted whether any of the ladies would have remembered packing them anyway. But because they had arrived late we now had them to put aside for Tim and Debbie, just a couple of days after the request had come in – how amazing!

The Lord had brought them in just at the right time. Not only that, but we felt also that as He looked down on us He was smiling, thinking, "I'm going to give you another lovely surprise when you open that box and find out that they are in fact children's masks and not for adults as you think."

Two wonderful surprises even before the day had properly begun. *Thank You Jesus!*

Dr Florea is well past retiring age but continues

to minister to the needs of poor children and has a special concern for Gypsy children. He is loved by many people and works so very hard. He also instructs young people in social work, and encourages them to look out for the needs of others. Professor Samu and Dr Mosora ably assist him in this work. We take many things over for Dr Florea and always he is so delighted at what we are able to bring. Everything is received with much joy.

Originally, he did not have enough chairs for his students to sit on so he made do with planks of wood stretched across the few chairs that he did have. We were able to take chairs over for him so that he was able to do away with the wood.

Every time, along with the other things, we take Bibles. He always needs them, especially for the evangelistic meetings that he holds in his clinic each week where he shares the gospel. It is salutary to think that he relies on what we are able to take him to carry out his work. We are so privileged to be a part of the great ministry exercised by these "beloved physicians."

CHAPTER 8

A Society in Need

It hardly needs saying that Romania after Ceausescu was a country with immense problems. Basic material provisions that we take for granted and throw away were regarded as luxuries. Situations that in our country would be considered as intolerable and provoke a public outcry had to be patiently borne there. While matters have improved since the tyrant's overthrow there is still a great deal to be desired. Some examples will illustrate just what I mean, and also demonstrate God's care and intervention.

We were once told by a hospital in this country that we could have two incubators. They were marked on the side "Obsolete" but we were not to worry. There was nothing wrong with them – it was just that a new type of machine had been introduced.

We picked them up, and on the lorry they went to go to Romania. We had no contact with a maternity hospital at that time, so as we drove around the country we asked if anyone knew of one. When we got to our Christian friends in Ploesti, they said that there was one in that town. So we left the incubators with them and carried on around the country.

We had not been home many days when we had a letter from our friends. Firstly, they said that the director of the maternity hospital was delighted to receive the incubators. Babies had been dying because there had not been enough to go around. Secondly, they wanted us to know that one of "our incubators" had actually saved a baby's life because it was battery-operated as well as functioning on the mains, which we did not know. A baby had needed to be taken to Bucharest and this incubator was the only battery-operated one they had. We were thrilled. Then the friends wrote further saying that because the director was so pleased with the machines from the West he wondered if their friends in the West could help with another problem. He took them to the back of the hospital and there in a dark room were thirty babies who had been abandoned by their mothers who had fled the hospital because they could not afford to look after them.

The smell in the room was absolutely terrible; many of the little ones did not have nappies – he did not have any and the cot sheets were filthy. They were also screaming because he did not have enough baby milk to give them, and furthermore he had no nurse to look after them. Was there any way that we could help?

Well, we knew that we could help with nappies, baby clothes and bedding, and we felt pretty sure too that if we asked on our needs list for money for baby milk that it would come in. That was alright, but our hearts sank because we knew that we did not have enough money to pay for a nurse to look after them, which was what they were asking. I was going to have to write and explain the situation.

However, the next day as Alan opened the post he discovered that we had been given an anonymous gift "to be used in whatever way you feel is right." As we looked at the amount we both realized that it was enough to pay a nurse's wage for six months.

We wrote immediately, "Yes, we can help with everything and employ a nurse. When we come we will bring her wages and do not worry about what will happen after six months. God is obviously in this and he will not let those babies down."

As others heard about the babies, they felt led to support them - so much so, that we were able to employ a night nurse as well. She, incidentally, found that the babies were being drugged in the night to prevent them crying.

The director also offered Carmen and Dorin a room at the hospital to counsel any further mothers who wanted to abandon their babies, persuading them that they would be helped with clothes, bedding and baby food. During this period they were able to persuade many mothers to take their babies home. It is a sign of the improvement of conditions among families in this part of Romania that this part of the work has now come to an end.

At a later date when we again went to pick up incubators, we were asked if we would like some feeding pumps; they were still in their boxes and were brand new. The doctor at the maternity hospital in Romania had not asked for them, but we felt that possibly he could use them, so we said yes. When we got to the warehouse both Alan and I were surprised to find that there were nine. We remarked at having (as we saw it) such an odd number. We thought perhaps that there would have been half a dozen or even ten or twelve. Nevertheless, we were grateful and they were put aside to be packed and labelled for the maternity hospital.

When we arrived on the next journey to the hospital, we unloaded all the things that we had for them, including the incubators and then passed the box with the feeding pumps in to the doctor, explaining that we didn't know if he needed them, and if he did, we were sorry, but there were only nine.

"Do I need them? Of course I do!" he exclaimed. "I have ten babies needing feeding pumps and I only have one. Nine is the exact number that I am needing!"

Alan and I looked at each other. We had thought what an odd number we had been given, but of course, it wasn't. God knew the exact number that was required!

It all began with two "obsolete" incubators, yet look what the Lord did.

We now needed to appeal for more money for baby milk so that we could support the maternity hospital. We asked for four thousand pounds and it came in.

Before this we had always asked for £1,800 and each time the money came in; one pound here, five pounds there, a ten-pound note elsewhere, and so on - there had never been any problem, and we were so grateful to all those who gave. But before one journey we had not even had one pound in for the milk. We could not understand it. This had never happened before and we knew that the milk was desperately needed. Equally, we knew that the Lord knew that also. We had to pray about this, so on the Friday we prayed asking the Lord to meet this urgent need.

On the Saturday, we had a telephone call from a lady in a church just outside Cardiff. She wanted to know if we would go to her house on the Tuesday night and speak to some young people. They met at the house every week and she was teaching them the importance of prayer. "I am sure that you have had answers to your prayers before," she said. "If you would share some of them with the young people I'm sure that it would be a great encouragement to them." We agreed to go, and so arrived at her house. I think we were both rather surprised at the age of the children. We expected teenagers but they were much younger, ranging from about six years old to twelve.

We shared with them some of the ways that we had seen God answer prayer, and then she said, "Now, is there anything that you would like the youngsters to pray for?"

We explained that we had no money for baby milk and said perhaps they could pray about that. We both presumed that when we were gone they would pray.

However, she immediately said, "Right, come on now boys and girls. On your knees and in your groups. You know what you have to pray for."

I was in a group where a little girl prayed so beautifully, "Dear God," she said, "I do not want the babies to die. Will you please make sure Alan and Ann get the money for baby milk?" I was so touched, and as we drove home, Alan said that a little boy in his group had prayed a similar prayer. We felt so blessed by being there.

Two days later Alan was the one who happened to open the post. He opened one envelope and said to me, "I can hardly believe what I am seeing." Inside the envelope was a letter from a couple who lived outside Cardiff. They said that the Lord had laid it on their hearts to send us some money for baby milk. Enclosed was a cheque for £1,800!

We know that God hears and answers even the prayers of little children, but to be shown this in such a remarkable way was truly amazing. You can imagine how these little children felt when they knew that within two days God had answered their prayers, which must have been so very special for them. These same children stood in the foyer of *Safeway* one Saturday afternoon and collected ten thousand bars of chocolate for us to take to Romania. They were learning that the Lord certainly does answer prayer. However, he wants us to work for his kingdom also. At a later date, they came with some older children to the warehouse to sing for us and pray for us before we left for Romania. They were certainly being instructed well in the things of God.

The prison at Gherla, where Pastor Richard Wurmbrand was imprisoned, has been one of the places that we have been visiting for quite a while. One of the prison officers had been converted and had permission from the director to invite our friend who was an evangelist. He had been allowed into this notorious prison for the first time and had been appalled at the situation he found there.

The blankets were falling apart; there was not enough bedding, and the men desperately needed clothes, shoes, underclothes, soap, toilet rolls and toothpaste. He had felt such compassion for them, many of them pushed into prison for minor things such as stealing to try and provide for their families. The prisons in Romania are tough, as you can imagine.

He contacted us and asked if we could help. We were not sure as we had no contact with any prisons at that time. However, on returning home there was a message from a prison offering us many different things for the charity. The Lord was one step ahead once again and we were delighted to be able to help at Gherla prison in some small way.

We had been thrilled when our evangelist friend shared with us how God was working there. One man who had become a Christian there in the prison, confessed that he had been a member of the *Securitate* (the state security service) and that he had tried to kill a pastor many years ago. He had arranged for the pastor's car to have an accident but fortunately he had survived and was now a politician in the Romanian government. The man now wanted to be baptized and requested that this pastor baptize him. What a day that was when the pastor met the man who had tried to murder him. He now joyfully baptized his brother in Christ.

We duly packed and took the things to Romania and were invited into the prison by the director. He said that he was going to bring in a number of men and asked if we would like to speak to them. We said, "Yes." We had a preacher with us and thought that it would be good if he gave a word. The men listened intently, most of them fairly young, but one older man caught my attention. As our friend shared the gospel I observed that this man's face was radiant and he was nodding vigorously in agreement. After the address this man slipped quietly forward and said that he had something to say. He told how he was in prison for murder, but although he was there for life, in his heart he was free. He had been forgiven by the Lord and now knew him as his own personal Saviour. Through visiting him in prison his daughter and son-in-law had come to the Lord also.

He then produced a hymnbook and sang, again his face full of joy. I was not the only one who shed a few tears. I noticed the men were affected also.

What a privilege we had been given in going there!

Our friend had spoken on the story of Zacchaeus. We had been given no indication beforehand that anyone was going to be asked to speak - the man himself did not know. However the Lord obviously did, and knew what he was going to speak on. This became clear to us as he spoke. Alan and I looked at each other in amazement. On the lorry we had 150 Romanian copies of Luke's Gospel where, of course, the story of Zacchaeus is recorded. We had been given them and had put them on the lorry looking to find a place for them. The Lord obviously had the prison in mind.

Lord, I never cease to be amazed at the way You work things out.

One day we had an letter from the Richard Wurmbrand School in a town called Iasi asking if we had any shelving in the warehouse, as they were badly in need of shelving to house the many books in the school. Unfortunately, we didn't have any shelving in the warehouse at that time.

However, amazingly the next day in the local newspaper we saw that an auction was to be held in a few days time and amongst the items for sale was just the shelving that was needed for the school.

Alan and another trustee went to the auction and stood there all day as the shelves that were for auction were being sold right at the end of the sale!

They came home delighted to have purchased them even though the price was more than they thought that they would have to pay, costing them £275. At that time we were not too well off with funds for the charity.

The very next day we were absolutely amazed to receive an anonymous gift through the post "to be used as needed". It was for £275 the exact amount that we had spent the day before.

Only Alan and myself and the other trustee knew that they were going to the auction to try and buy the shelving. The shelving wasn't bought and the £275 paid, until very late the previous afternoon and yet first thing in the morning we had sent to us the exact amount. The Lord was at work yet again!

The Lord's timing is always perfect. We have read that in the Bible, but have been shown that it is true over and over again. Baby milk delivered to the baby orphanage just at the right time - they had run out the previous day - money given us to take to Dr Vali, arriving just at the right time . . . we could go on and on. What an encouragement it has been to us to see God at work in this way!

Let me tell you another remarkable story. We have continually supported an old people's home in Moldavia, in the north-east of Romania. When we first visited this place we were horrified; many of the old people had no underclothes, no shoes, and hardly any bedding on their beds. The little they did have was being washed by hand in cold water. Men and women were in together – many of them in a cold, dark, dank basement with hardly any light. They were desperately short of food and other necessities such as soap and toilet paper.

Even sadder was the fact that in with these people were young people of only 23. They were there because if you are that age and still in an orphanage you have to go to the nearest old people's home. What hope did they have of a future? So, feeling touched by the whole situation, we had taken over washing machines and dryers and many other things that were needed. We had been so pleased a few years before when they had been given a "newer" building by the state. They could not move in however, because there was no heating and the state had no money. But the Lord was good and we were able to supply what was needed and together with Romanian Christians were able to install heating there, so that the old people could finally move in.

Once they were in we realized that they had gone from having hardly any windows to rooms where there were large expanses of glass. Without curtains the heat would make it impossible for them to stay in the rooms in the summer.

We knew that curtains and curtain material would be expensive, so started searching for cheap material. We eventually found a firm which let us have Marks & Spencer curtain material for fifty pence a yard. We were so grateful but we realized that it was going to be costly to have the curtains made. Then we remembered a Christian friend in Milton Keynes who did a lot of sewing, so we rang her up and asked her if she would be prepared to get a team of ladies from her church together to make up the curtains. She was delighted to be asked and so together they made up over 200 metres of material into curtains.

We then asked her if she and her husband would be willing to come to Romania with us to fit the curtains if we got a few men to help them. I had already written to Swish Integra asking them if they had any cheap track that we could have and they had very generously given us enough track without any charge. We thought that the men could fix the track and our friend the curtains. They both said yes and so these people in their seventies climbed aboard our lorry for the journey to

Romania. We dropped them at the old people's home and Alan and I went off around the country picking up the team on the way back. They had done a marvellous job, and the place looked more like a home than an institution when they finished.

That particular journey was one of our bad ones. We were kept on the Romanian border from eight o'clock at night until four o'clock the following morning. The mosquitoes were terrible and we were all badly bitten. One of our party had to phone his doctor friend at home for advice because he was so ill.

I said to Alan on the return journey, "That's the last job this couple will ever do for us." Not so, they were absolutely brilliant and were eager to be used if necessary again. We have used them many times since for particular jobs and they are a joy to have with us, even though they are now aged 80 and 77.

Thank You, Lord, that when people have a heart for You and Your work You will always find them a job to do no matter what their age.

On another occasion we had taken a new volunteer to the home and he was mortified when he saw the state of the cooking stove. We knew it was bad but it worked most of the time. When it didn't, their meals came four and a half miles by horse and cart. As you can imagine they were always stone cold. We had been able to sort out the heating for them but finances would not run to a new stove as we knew that a re-conditioned catering stove would cost about a thousand pounds. This man, however, had a friend who was quite wealthy and would, he felt, be willing to give the money for the stove. He said he would contact him on returning home. Sure enough, a few days after returning home he rang to say that his friend would be happy to pay for a stove and told us to go ahead and order one. So Alan and another trustee found a commercial electric stove for a thousand pounds and asked the man to keep it for us, as at that time there was no room in the warehouse. We would collect it and pay for it just before we went. The man was happy to oblige.

A few months later we had a telephone call from a lady who was on our mailing list. "I know that you do not want clothes," she said, "but I passed your leaflet on to a neighbour for her to read. She is housebound and very lonely so I thought she might find it interesting. The trouble is she has now telephoned to say that she has sorted out some black bags of clothes for you and I didn't like to say anything because it had obviously been an effort for her to put these things together. Do you think you could pick them up? I'm so sorry to cause this problem."

Well we understood perfectly and so arranged to call at the lady's house to pick them up. As we were driving there I said to Alan, "We will soon be off to Romania. You will need to go and pay for that stove for the old people's home and bring it back to the warehouse." Alan's face fell. "Ann, I haven't had time to tell you. I only heard yesterday the man who was going to pay for the stove has a problem and he can no longer buy it for us."

I could not believe it. We both felt awful. Not only had the supplier kindly kept it for us but also we had told the director of the old people's home that we would be bringing one out. What a bad witness it was to both of them! What on earth were we going to do?

"Well, there is no money in *Support for Romania* to buy it," Alan said; then, as we neared the house,

"We'll just have to discuss it later."

Into the house we went and sat for a little while talking to the lady. She had obviously led quite a full social life and was feeling cut off from everything. It was good to be able to talk to her, but then it was time to pick up the bags and leave.

As we got up to go she asked, "What is the name of your charity, by the way? I know it was on the literature but I've forgotten." So we told her and then she said, "I'd like to give you a cheque for your work." We said, "No, please, we don't expect that. We are glad to have met you and to have the clothes."

"No, no," she returned, "I want to give you a cheque," getting her cheque-book from her bag and beginning to write. She then handed me the cheque. So I said thank you, and popped it in my bag, obviously without looking at it. We then said our goodbyes. When we arrived home I gave Alan the cheque to put through the books and went out of the room. He called after me, "Ann, did you know how much the cheque was for?"

"Of course not, why should I?"

"Well, you had better come and have a look." I did, and the cheque was for a thousand pounds – the exact amount of money to pay for the stove.

Thank You, Lord, that even as Alan and I talked about the problem, it was no problem to You because You had already sorted it all out.

Is it any wonder that we count it as a joy and a privilege to be allowed to work alongside the Lord? He constantly amazes and surprises us.

One of the wonderful successes that has been achieved is the training of many Christian young people in Social Work. They have graduated, and many are now working in the city of Oradea among the homeless, mentally ill, terminally ill, street children, old people, prostitutes and single mothers. A Christian lady from a church in Cardiff, who lived in Romania for four years, trained these young people. She was not a well person and at times found it very difficult, but the Lord has certainly used her and today those social workers are doing wonderful work there in Oradea. They regularly send us reports of their work and we have been amazed at what God has done in just that area.

We take many things out for the social workers including drugs, medicines, creams and bandages. These are donated by individuals, doctors' surgeries and hospitals and are sorted out in our warehouse by a team of Christian doctors. When funds allow, we also buy new drugs for this very important work. Let me share just one story.

One day we had an SOS by fax. The social workers were desperately in need of a syringe driver. At that point we did not know what that was but were then told that it was an automatic device for administering pain relief to the terminally ill. We decided to send away to the Christian medical firm that we use.

We received the syringe driver safely, together with a bill for £650. We were astounded. We honestly did not realize that it was so expensive and did not have the money to pay the bill. We then remembered a lady in a church that we knew who was a social worker and rang her asking her if she could possibly explain to her church the situation and the importance of the syringe driver, asking them if they could help out. She did, and in one day the money came in.

How the Lord has used that syringe driver! He

has taken something very ordinary and done more than we could ever have thought, or imagined.

There was a young man called Sebastian who loved sport and had aspirations to be a doctor. He was suddenly struck down with cancer of the femur. In Romania, if you are terminally ill, you are virtually sent home to die, often without any care or medication; there are no MacMillan nurses or Marie Curie homes! The social workers heard about Sebastian and visited his home, where his mother was doing her best to look after him. He was an angry and bitter young man and was very hostile to the social workers and doctor who visited him. They offered to use the syringe driver on him to help with the pain. At first he refused, not wanting anything to do with them, but after gentle persuasion on their part, he gave in and allowed them to treat him.

Over the months the social workers spoke to Sebastian telling him that cancer could destroy the body but not the soul and explained the good news about Jesus. Before Sebastian died, he came to know the Lord Jesus Christ as his own personal Saviour and knew he was going to heaven. Isn't that wonderful and so encouraging for us? After Sebastian's death his mother started going to church.

Those working with the terminally ill needed a building where they could provide day respite care for their patients. They were able, with our help, to purchase a building for this purpose. It was badly in need of refurbishment and we were able to supply the materials and take them over

Romanian builders completed the work and then we sent over a team to plaster paint and decorate the building. What a joy it was for two of our trustees to be with them for the opening in October 2005.

These social workers are doing such a wonderful work amongst the terminally ill including supporting and visiting them in their own homes.

Their vision is now to have a building where they can provide day and night care for those who are so very ill.

Below we have shown one of many letters that the hospice team have received from those who have been so grateful for the help that they have given.

My name is Claudia Veres and my mother was terminally ill with cancer. We contacted the Emanuel Hospice and soon afterwards the doctor and one of the nurses came to the house to assess the situation. They were God's Angels in disguise for our entire family during this difficult time. They visited our house nearly every day during the winter. It didn't matter how bad the weather was. When she needed stronger medication they went out of their way to get it for her. My mother was comforted in her pain and she was able to spend her last days surrounded by her family. My mother wanted to spend the little time she had left at home and not in a hospital bed. Thank you Emanuel Hospice, for being God's messengers to my family, and for making my mother's departure easier. Thank you for representing Jesus whilst doing your job! I am reminded of the verse in Matthew 25 vs. 36-40 where Jesus identifies himself with the sick people. 'I was sick and you visited me' and the righteous asked the Lord 'When did we see you sick and go to visit you?' and the Lord replies 'I tell you the truth whatever you did for one of the least of these brothers (or sisters) of mine, you did it for me'

What a lovely letter and what a tribute to Emanuel Hospice who work with the terminally ill.

We take many things for the kindergartens which many churches are opening, finding it a really good means of outreach as many of the children come from non-Christian families. We have been told many times of how the parents have come to the monthly meetings which are held, to receive an update on their children's progress, and as the gospel is shared also, many parents have come to the Lord. "Be assured," we are told, "you bring toys and games for us and of course, the children are delighted and they are a great help to us, but the Lord uses the things that you bring as a means of bringing people to Himself."

Another couple who we regularly support are Florin and Antoanina who are ministering to the sewer children. These children who are homeless live under the ground in the sewers. Their horrific plight featured recently in a BBC *Newsnight* programme.

Caring for these children is hard and can be quite dangerous as those who do so are frequently threatened by men who use many of these young children and teenagers as prostitutes.

Florin and Antoanina are doing a wonderful work, not only feeding and clothing these youngsters but watching out for their health and providing shelter for those who are desperately trying to escape from the hands of these men and turn their lives around. They also share about Jesus with them as they show God's love in action. We take many things over for this couple's ministry as they have so little to work with themselves and are grateful for all that we are able to provide.

They have told us of the harrowing situations in the sewers, with disease brought by the many rats living there, and the burns that many of the children have received from the underground hot water pipes that run through there.

It is a very special ministry and we are full of admiration for them as they seek to serve the Lord in this way.

CHAPTER 9

Four Churches

The first is in a town called Chisineu Cris where we became very involved in the building of a church. Alan had been involved with three Romanians through the Romanian Missionary Society, who had come to Wales to study theology. They had gone to various churches to preach and then when qualified had returned to Romania. One of the young men went back to pastor a church. The people were meeting in a Hungarian church, whose premises they were sharing, and they badly needed a building of their own. The many churches with which he had built up a friendship whilst in Britain decided to help him and started sending us money to take over for him. However, as he pointed out to us, many of the materials that were needed were unobtainable there, and he asked if we could buy them and take them over, which we did. I think that we took practically everything that was needed for that church (including things for the interior) and also finally a man to lay the carpet and tile the huge hall that was to be used for weddings. He freely gave of his time and did a magnificent job.

It was so encouraging for us to have so many eager hands always waiting to unload whatever we had brought, and very moving to see both the men and the ladies building the church together, often working late in the evenings by arc lights. Many of them came straight from their work and also gave up their holidays so that they could help with the construction.

What a joy it was to be able to go over for the official opening of that church! We took two coaches because so many who had so generously given wanted to be there. It was a great privilege to be involved in this project, but we both felt that this was a one-off. With all our other work, it would have been very, very hard to do it again; it would be just too much. The Lord has since truly blessed this young man's ministry.

The second church that we have been very impressed with is in a village called Calacea. It was built without permission in Communist times. It was almost completed when the *Securitate* heard about it and sent bulldozers down from the city of Oradea to bulldoze it to the ground. Christians heard that they were coming and congregated inside the church. When they came they refused to leave saying, "Bulldoze the church if you wish, but you bulldoze us as well, because we are not coming out," and they prayed and sang at the top of their voices. The men on the bulldozers eventually gave up and returned to Oradea and never came back. Today it is a flourishing church, with great influence in the village.

The pastor, a godly Spirit-filled man, has now converted an old building (with help from the U.S.A.) about thirty metres away from the church, into a medical centre. There he has not only a doctor, but a dentist and a children's clinic and other facilities. There are three other villages next to Calacea and there was not a doctor between them. There was only one telephone and that was not always working. The nearest city, Oradea, is 25 miles away. Can you imagine what you would have done if you were taken ill, especially if you were elderly, or had young children? What chance would you stand if you had to be taken 25 miles mostly over really rough roads with no lighting?

Prior to the building's completion, Pastor Radu Tets showed us around and he pointed out to us what the various rooms would be used for. "It will be a Christian Medical Centre," he said. "There will be Christian music, Christians working here, Christian literature; this will be a place where Jesus is."

"But, Radu, where will everything come from, all the equipment, all the furnishings? You need so many things and we know that you have no money?"

He looked at us in astonishment. "From the Lord, of course. He gave me the vision, so He will provide everything." He put his hands in the air. "Thank You, Jesus. I'm so excited at what You are going to do here." It is at times like this one feels very small. As Alan said later, "Sometimes it makes you feel as though you have only just begun the Christian life. We have so much to learn from these dear people, who truly know what it means to live by faith."

This medical centre has now opened. We take many things for the work there – medicines, a dentist's chair, lawn seed to grass the outside area. In the waiting room are brand new Parker-Knoll moquette chairs which we were told were going on a skip and which we hurriedly rescued.

On one of our journeys Pastor Radu asked if it would be possible when we returned to fit a sound-system in the clinic because it was so quiet while people were waiting and he would like to play Christian music. This we were able to provide and at a later date he asked if we could bring an antenna in order to pick up the 24-hour Christian radio from Oradea.

Using donations we bought a sound-system and an aerial, and on our next journey some of our team fitted it for him. He was delighted and shortly after our return wrote to say that people who were not ill were coming into the clinic and sitting in the waiting room just to hear the music and the Gospel message put out by the Christian radio. Who knows what God will accomplish there?

We were inspired by this brother's vision and since the medical centre has opened, we take many things for him regularly. He has recently had the joy of baptizing twenty new Christians in his church.

Praise the Lord for men like Pastor Radu who himself has a remarkable testimony of how when he was six years old the Lord had spoken to him about being a preacher.

A little while later, on one of our visits, Radu informed us that he was now going to build a new church in a village called Magesti. "It is a small village," he said. "There is no church there and also no known Christians." We were astonished at such a bold venture, but Radu was adamant that the Lord had called him to do this and so the venture could not fail. As the church was being built he went around the houses in the village introducing himself and taking shoeboxes to the children at Christmas, and Easter eggs which we had supplied. He was building up relationships with the people. (Incidentally, we took over 18,000 Easter eggs on that particular journey).

On the day of the opening of the church, Radu took the brass band and choir from his other church and the building was packed. He has since held many baptismal services for people who have come to know the Lord and the fellowship is growing rapidly.

There is another large church in the city of Oradea that holds three thousand people. This was built mainly with money from America and is very impressive. They have a medical centre and a dental surgery. We actually transported the whole dental surgery that was given us by a dentist in Cardiff, who was refurbishing his practice. They also have a Christian university, a high school and a kindergarten as well as an orphanage made up of a number of houses, each one having a "Mum and Dad" and ten children making a family unit. They were built by a Swedish Pentecostal Church. We have also taken many things for this church.

Let me tell you of a third church that we visited. Alan and I were on our own in Romania. We had gone by car as there were a few problems that we had to deal with that we could not do in convoy.

Our friend Matiu asked us if we would like to visit a Gypsy church in a local village. The pastor was a friend of his and there was going to be a baptism of eighteen people. Interestingly enough, this pastor had been converted under the ministry of Radu Tets.

We were delighted; what a wonderful experience that would be for us! We set off on the Sunday morning. His service started, we were told, at 10.30 am. We arrived in the village to see that the church was actually a small house. Many people were outside and we managed to get through to the open door. Inside, two rooms had obviously been knocked into one but even then the space was small. In that space were two hundred people (Alan counted them!); all but a few were standing, the rest were sitting on wooden benches in the front. Together with Matiu and his wife and two daughters we were put as honoured guests on the benches, seats which people had given up for us.

The people sitting on the benches were those who were to be baptized and they were all in white. I could see that it had obviously been a struggle for many of them to do this, observing blouses held together with safety pins, white shirts frayed at the collar and mostly broken white plimsolls on their feet. Many of them were middle-aged or elderly.

The Gypsy pastor started preaching. We were fortunate that Matiu's two daughters spoke fluent English and so were able to interpret for us. He preached powerfully and as I sat and listened I noticed his emerald green suit, bright blue, green and red kipper tie, and pink shirt, frayed at the collar. My eyes went to his feet, taking in the black shoes which had seen better days, complete with brown laces.   For some reason I felt so moved by this and felt tears well up within me.

He then announced that anyone who wanted to pray or praise the Lord should do so, and furthermore asked Alan and myself to sing. We felt it would have been churlish to refuse, so sang a duet together after one of the daughters explained the words to the congregation. Mind you, we have sung a duet before in another church and when we returned months later they wanted us to sing again. I suppose that is well and good if you have a good voice. Alan has, but I haven't. Nevertheless, my heart is in the right place!

After we had sung our chorus, a young man stood up at the back of the church, closed his eyes, threw his head back and sang also. As he did so, a man started playing an accordion at the front. The young man sang his heart out for all of five minutes as the accordion accompanied him.   Later I was to say to Alan, "I know that I'm not musical but did that young man sing out of tune? It sounded funny to me."

"Not only was he singing out of tune," Alan laughed, "but the accordion was being played in a different key." No wonder even I thought it didn't sound right, but what did it matter? They were praising the Lord with all their might!

Before the baptism, all the candidates gave their testimonies and what testimonies they were! Some had been in prison, some had been alcoholics, but the Lord had wonderfully saved them. What a joy it was to hear how lives had been changed! Matiu explained later that these dear people were having a great impact in the villages where they lived. The fact is that the Gypsies in Romania have a very bad name for stealing, lying and living in squalor. Now the other villagers could see how their lives had changed and what a difference Jesus makes.

Then came the baptism – in the back garden. There was snow on the ground, it was minus twenty degrees and they had a bath-sized plastic tub of water in which they were going to baptize the people. In the Baptist tradition believing adults are normally fully immersed. This tub did not seem big enough for the job but with great difficulty it was achieved. This they did to more joyful singing. We had to leave after seeing only a couple of baptisms as it was two o'clock and they had only just started. The service had already been three and a half hours long.

On the way home I said to Alan, "Did you notice that young man's accordion how it was held together with brown tape and string?" Alan had, and said, "Wouldn't it be good if we could get a better one for him." I agreed, but knew that in fourteen years we had only ever had one accordion come in to the warehouse.

When we returned home, there was a message on our answerphone asking if we could use an accordion! Could we? Of course we could! We knew the exact place where it was needed.

Let me tell you about the fourth church, the honey church. On one of our visits to a family the man of the house asked us if we would go into the back garden because he had something to show us. We went around and saw dozens and dozens of beehives. The brother explained that there was a group of Christians in the village but they had no church in which to worship. They obviously could not afford to pay anyone to build a church and could not, anyway, afford the materials. However, he had an idea. Did we think that we could take the honey back to sell it for him? He could then use the money to buy building materials and the Christians, both men and women, would build the church. We were impressed. It seemed a wonderful idea, but would it work? Well, we could but try. So we started bringing back aluminium churns (like the old milk churns) full of honey for this man.

On arriving home we put out an SOS. "Is there anyone who would be willing to jar-up this honey for us and sell it?" Well, we waited a while and then a Christian lady rang us. She was not in good health and could not get out much, but she said, "This is something that I can do for the Lord." So she started potting up the honey in her own home. She also got her son to make labels on his computer saying "Romanian Honey," and started selling it.

It sold like the proverbial hot cakes. It was pure honey, no additives or preservatives, and people loved it, and kept coming back for more. So we had to bring back more and more honey to satisfy the demand and, of course, this meant more and more money for the honey man.

Many journeys later as we took the honey man yet more money he asked us to go the middle of the village. There stood the church almost completed, built with the money from the honey. We were so moved and were able to take photographs to show the lady. She was thrilled that she had been able to help the Lord build a church in Romania.

As the honey sales increased so many more people have sold honey for us.

Thank You Lord, that when we do something for You, no matter how small or ordinary, in Your hands it becomes big.

CHAPTER 10

Deliverance, Intervention, Protection

We were being followed!

Alan and I were travelling on our own when we noticed a particular car on our tail. The car eventually overtook us and stopped us. We locked the lorry and waited while two burly men came to Alan's window. They spoke to Alan in broken English asking where we were going. Alan told them.

"Ah, I know a quicker way," said the man, "you just follow me."

"No," said Alan, "we know this way and we are fine."

"No, no. Follow us," they said. Then threateningly, "we insist you follow us," and they got back into their car, slowly driving in front of us.

I was petrified but thought I must not show it. "Who are they?" I timidly asked Alan.

"I don't know," he answered calmly, "but don't worry, it's okay. I'm going to hang back a bit and then shoot off a side road and try and lose them. It's alright," he said, looking at my face, "they're probably only trying to be helpful, but just to be on the safe side we will turn off when we can."

I prayed silently to the Lord, "Please, Lord, keep us safe, watch over us and protect us."

The car had pulled a little further ahead and at the next side road Alan veered off. "Thank goodness for that," he said, with evident relief. "Better to be safe than sorry."

I breathed a sigh of relief and settled back. Then, as we rejoined the main road, I saw the car waiting for us. Again, Alan was so calm. "It's alright," he assured me, "I told you not to worry." I quietly started to pray again frantically - I was really, really scared. Neither of us said a word as we drove along, until suddenly without any warning Alan veered off the road again, going through back street after back street.

We eventually would have to come out on the other road, even if it was miles further on. As we approached it, my heart was in my mouth. I stole a look at Alan. He smiled at me - he was so calm. Why was I like this? I really shouldn't be.

We got nearer and nearer to the other road and when we came out, we looked all around. No car! "Are you sure?" I asked Alan. "Could it be hiding?"

"No, I don't think so," he said, "they've gone, we are alright now. They've obviously given up."

As we drove along, I said to Alan, "You know, I was absolutely petrified, but I didn't want to show it. You were so calm, I felt ashamed."

"Ann, I was really scared too", he replied, "but I didn't want to worry you."

"Oh, Alan, the Lord has protected us," I said. "I was praying all the time."

"Ann," said Alan, "so was I!"

We told the people at our next destination about the men in the car. "You were very fortunate," they said. "Men like that have been stopping foreign lorries and offering to show them a quicker way. When the people have followed them, they lead them to a quiet place where a gang is waiting to rob them and beat them up. Sometimes if the people refuse to follow them they take a chance and do it in the open anyway. Sometimes they have knives and even guns."

Thank You, Lord, for answering our prayers once again - not only ours, but the prayers of Your people at home who so faithfully remember us.

We always send out itineraries so that people can pray.

I was not with Alan when he pulled into a garage with his co-driver for diesel. As he got out of the cab a shifty-looking man came up to him and asked him if he wanted to change money. Alan said no, knowing all about these men, many of whom are crooks who frequently target westerners.

As he went to the pump the man went around to the passenger side. Alan called to his co-driver, "Just keep saying no until he goes away."

Alan filled up the lorry and went in to pay, and as he came out of the office, he saw a man walking quickly to a car with a briefcase under his arm. That looks like my briefcase, thought Alan. That is my briefcase! He started to run after the man, who also started to run and then jumped in a car that sped off at high speed. Alan was devastated; inside that briefcase were the passports, his credit cards, a thousand pounds in notes and important documents and papers.

What had happened was that as the one man kept the co-driver talking, his accomplice had reached through the driver's window and stolen the briefcase. Alan ran back to the office shouting to the man there telling him what had happened and asking him to telephone the police, only to feel that he too was probably in on this racket because he pretended that he did not understand and certainly did not want to know. There was nothing to do but telephone our friend in Oradea and ask him to come out to the garage so that Alan could explain to him and he could phone the police. So he got hold of Matiu who promised to come out, which would take about fifteen minutes.

Alan was in a terrible state; he realized the consequences of having no passport, no visas, no credit cards, and also losing the money which he needed to pass on to people. He got back in the driver's seat and put his head in his hands. The co-driver was also upset, knowing how he had been tricked.

"Lord, what am I going to do, how am I going to be able to cope with all this?" he prayed. As he lifted his head he was aware of a man who was putting diesel in a car at the side of the lorry. He was looking at Alan and pointing vigorously to the front of the truck. Alan stared at him not understanding what he was trying to convey. The man was pointing again, over and over, at the front of the truck.

Alan decided that he had better get out of the lorry to see what he was pointing at. What was the problem? As he went to the front of the truck, he did a double- take; his briefcase was standing there in front of the bumper. He gingerly picked it up and looked towards the man with the car but he had gone.

He took it into the cab of the lorry and opened it. Every single thing was intact-passports, credit cards, visas - even the thousand pounds was all there.

Alan and his co-driver looked at each other in absolute amazement. It was such a small garage, they would have seen a car draw up and somebody

Dr Vali and his wife Jeni.

Adi, the young man who was
rescued by Dr Vali and his wife,
is now in Bible college.

Alan receives a plaque from Dr
Vali thanking the charity for
their support over many years.

Tim and Debbie who now live in
Romania stand with the twins
they have been fostering with a
view to adoption.

Unloading fruit at Dr Vali's
which was kindly donated by the
Wholesale Fruit Centre, Cardiff.

Dr Florea used planks of wood for his meetings until we took out extra chairs for him.

Alan receives a banner made for us by one of the Kindergartens we support.

Carmen supervises the unloading of incubators that we have delivered to the maternity hospital in Ploiesti.

Some of the children in the orphanage. Note how close together the cots are.

Prisoners at Gherla prison unload blankets from our truck.

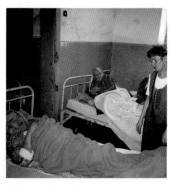

This is the Old People's in Siret home before they were given a newer building. Isn't it sad?

Some of the men in the Old People's home - notice how young some of them are.

Putting up curtains in Siret that were made by ladies in Milton Keynes and Cardiff. Previously they had none.

The boilers we purchased for the Old People's home. Our Romanian friend Sami helped to install them.

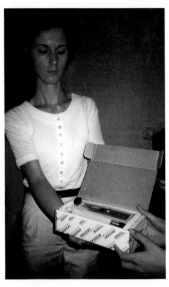

Dr Mihaela, one of the team at Emanuel Hospice, receives the syringe driver for their work with the terminally ill.

The Emanuel Hospice building in which we had a large involvement.

Florin and Antonina who work with the sewer children in Bucharest

Street children huddling together by a ventilation shaft in order to keep warm.

Pastor Radu Tet, a man of vision.

These pews from Swindon were taken to Magesti church where the ladies recovered them.

Emanuel Church, Oradea, which holds 3500 people and is full most Sundays.

Rev Gareth Evans leading one of our services in Ararat Baptist prior to leaving for Romania.

Baptismal candidates waiting to be baptized in the garden of the Gypsy church.

'The Honey Man' stands with his grandson

The money from his honey built this church.

When a well-known local ironmonger's shop closed after nearly a century we were told that we could have all the contents!! What a job it was for us to clear it, but the many things that were there were a great help to many people.

One of the families who lost their house due to the flooding in April 2005. We continue to send help there.

One of the houses in Rast, Romania, destroyed by the floods of April 2005. They were desperately poor already and now this!

place it there. So how had it got there? The last Alan had seen of it was when it disappeared into a car which had sped away.

"It was a complete and utter mystery," said Alan, when he told me the story later.

"I know what happened," I said. "An angel snatched it from their car and brought it back and placed it there. It's the only explanation."

Alan said nothing. He was totally bewildered by the whole episode. I don't think he agreed with me but what other explanation was there? The Lord knew how important all those things were in the briefcase. Again, is there anything too hard for the Lord? – of course not.

When I think of the next story I think of Balaam's ass, and how the Lord used such an animal for His purposes. (Numbers 22) He does use many things to accomplish His plans, doesn't He? Let me tell you how He used a crowd of Gypsies.

We had been travelling a long time leaving one town and on our way to another. For various reasons we had been unable to eat or drink. Because of this we were all feeling weary and were on the look-out for a safe place to stop. You have to be careful where you stop in Romania and not take any chances. We eventually found a quiet spot and all the trucks parked at the side of the road. Out came the kettles, tea and coffee - we were so longing for something to eat and drink.

Suddenly, I heard one of the men say, "Oh, no," and looking up I saw dozens and dozens of Gypsies advancing towards us. Where they appeared from I will never know, but appear they did. We knew that it was impossible to stay now, because many Gypsies are never ever satisfied, no matter what you give them. They keep on and on and can get quite nasty when you finally refuse. So we quickly packed up everything. We were all thoroughly fed up, wondering if we would find another place and would be travelling for another couple of hours.

Off the convoy went until about forty minutes later when Alan spotted a place just off the side of the main road. It looked as though it would be alright. We hoped that it would be, so Alan signalled for the lorries to follow him and pull over. We parked up and again got out everything that was needed.

I was at the rear of the front lorry boiling the kettle, when one of the men came along with a young lady carrying a baby. "This young lady has just appeared at the rear of our lorry," he said. "She has some money clutched in her hand. She speaks a little English, and wants to know if we have any baby clothes on the lorries that we can sell her." I smiled at her as she looked so pathetic and yet had a sweet face. We did have some clothes on the lorries and we took off two large boxes, which the men put into her old car. She tried to press the money into my hand saying with tears in her eyes, "Thank you, thank you, you are so good."

"Please," I responded, "we don't want payment. We are glad to be able to help you," and not wanting her to continue to think that we were good, asked her to wait a minute. I returned to the cab of the lorry and pulled out a *Journey into Life* in Romanian (this little booklet shares the gospel in a very simple way). I pressed it gently into her hand. "You know, only God is good, that is why we do His work, because He has been so good to us."

She looked at the book with amazement. "You are Christians! So am I. You know I had no clothes for my baby. I had this little money, but baby clothes are so hard to find in Romania. This morning I prayed to the Lord that somehow He would lead me to a place where I could buy some baby clothes. As I passed on the road, I saw your lorries and thought, well, maybe you would have some clothes on board, and you did. Also you are Christians and you have given them to me freely."

Later that night as Alan and I reviewed the day we talked about Maria, for that was her name. We looked at each other, knowing what we had both just realized. God had brought those Gypsies to move us on. He had arranged an appointment for a young lady, and for us. We needed to be in the right place at the right time so that she would see us as she passed. What is more she would have turned off the main road well before our first stop where we had encountered the Gypsies.

Thank You, Lord, once again, for showing us that You arrange in our lives from time to time divine appointments and You will let nothing stand in Your way.

Maria gave us her address and whenever we pass through her village we call in and she insists on giving us a meal. Her little baby has grown and is a young boy now, but we will never forget how we met them.

Let me share with you another appointment that the Lord arranged for Alan and me.

It was near Christmas time and Alan had asked me to go to a post office a little way from the warehouse to buy eight hundred second-class stamps. We were due to send out the mailing to our supporters. I dutifully drove to the post office and came back with the stamps, handing them to Alan. His face fell. "Oh, no," he exclaimed, "Why did you get these?"

"Well, they're the ones you asked for. They're second-class and there are eight hundred there."

"Yes, but look at them, they're Christmas stamps."

"Well, that doesn't matter, does it? There is nothing wrong with using them."

"Of course there is. Christmas stamps are bigger than ordinary ones and we now have three times the area to lick."

I looked at him in astonishment, marvelling at how his mind works, although I could see that he had a point. "It's alright," he said, turning away, "we'll just have to use these." I could tell by his face that he was not happy, so I volunteered, "Look, don't worry, I'll take them back and change them for some ordinary ones. I know you'll be happier with that."

We only had one vehicle that day because the van was in for repair, so Alan said, "Well, if you like, I'll come with you. I've forgotten something at the house; we can call there first, collect it and then go on to the post office." I was secretly pleased, thinking that he could come in and explain about the stamps.

We got in the car, Alan driving. As we eventually got to the end of our road, instead of turning in, Alan went straight on.

"I thought you were going to the house," I said.

"Well, I was, but I've changed my mind, I think we'll go to the post office first." I didn't mind; it didn't make any difference to me. We parked outside the post office and we both went inside.

There was an elderly lady talking to the man behind the counter. We waited behind her. "I was wondering if you could tell me where the nearest police station or church is?" she was asking.

The man behind the counter sighed, "Well, I've only just taken over here, so I'm afraid I can't be much help. There is a church further down the road, but I don't know about the police station."

We both knew where the police station was so Alan said, "Excuse me, but I can tell you where the police station is," and he carefully explained how to get there.

She thanked him, and then said, "I only asked about the church and police station actually because I thought that they may be able to help me. You see, I'm looking for a man who goes to Romania, but I don't know how to find him." Alan and I looked at each other and then Alan said, "Would his name be Alan Penrose by any chance?" The lady looked at him in amazement. "Yes, that's right." "Well." said Alan, "I'm that man."

I can still see the shock on the lady's face as she said in wonder, "I don't believe it."

Then she told us her story. She had been asked by friends to help transport goods from Derby to our warehouse and she had willingly agreed. They could not get everything in their car, so she had filled her car also. The friends had brought things to us before so they knew exactly where to come. She was happy to follow them knowing that they knew the way. However, it did not quite work out as she planned. She had lost them between Monmouth and Newport, so had arrived in Cardiff, having no idea of where she was to go. She had arrived at the post office really upset knowing only the name of a man who went to Romania.

We were stunned, hardly able to believe it ourselves that we had arrived just at the right time for this lady. The Lord had watched over her and helped her.

When Alan and I talked about it later, I said to him, "You know, if you had gone to the house first as you'd planned, we probably would have missed that lady, and," I added with a grin, "if I hadn't got the stamps wrong we wouldn't have had to go back."

"Alright, alright," he laughed, "you've made your point."

Over and over again we have said to each other that so often we look for God in the big things, and quite rightly so because He is God, but for us the miracle is that He is in the ordinary things of life as well, guiding and helping us day by day.

CHAPTER 11

Unusual Gifts

So many different things are taken to Romania from the warehouse - even a batch of right footed shoes for left foot amputees – and other unusual items that have been a little too large for the warehouse such as caravans (for Christian camps), canoes, a whole dental surgery and even a combine harvester. We have certainly taken over a variety of items. We take many things over for Christian camps that are held throughout the country - tents, sleeping-bags, food, fold-up beds, cooking utensils etc. We were also given six canoes in excellent condition and they went to a Crusaders Camp. Many young people were converted at that camp and again we rejoice that the Lord enabled us to help in a practical way.

We have even taken three caravans so that the helpers can sleep a little more comfortably. These have been towed on the back of our van - making sure that they were filled to capacity first of course!!

We have taken over many wedding dresses. There are not many wedding dresses for sale in Romania and those that are there are too expensive for anyone to buy. We take them to the pastors of various churches. They keep them in stock, as it were, and they are then lent out to the brides, who return them after the wedding so that they can be used again.

Here's the story of one of those wedding dresses. We were visiting a local church that has faithfully supported us and the preacher requested that Alan go forward and tell the congregation of any special need that had not as yet been met for our next journey, which was only weeks away.

Alan said, "Well, actually there is only one thing, and that is a wedding dress for a very poor family whose daughter is getting married and they haven't got a dress." And he gave the size that was needed. The minister then said to Alan, "Before you sit down perhaps you would like to pray that God will supply that need for you." So he prayed that indeed the Lord would find someone who had a wedding dress that they were willing to give and that it would be the right size.

He opened his eyes and made to sit down when an elderly lady jumped up shouting, "My daughter's got a wedding dress that size. It's at home, I'm going off to get it," and with that she practically ran out of the door. Amidst much laughter the minister shouted, "Don't forget to come back for the sermon!"

She did come back, triumphantly carrying the wedding dress. Interestingly enough, as she got into her hallway her daughter was at the top of the stairs with the wedding dress in her hand. She had just that minute been looking at it.

We were later told how thrilled that lady was to know that she had the dress that was needed in Romania. Although elderly, she had not been a Christian for long and told many people how the Lord had used her.

We were once given a most exquisite wedding dress which had never been worn and had cost a thousand pounds. One absolutely delighted young Romanian lady had the honour of wearing it. She sent a photograph of herself in the dress to the lady who had kindly given it, thanking her for making her day so very special with "the most beautiful dress that I have ever seen."

Of course, as more and more people hear of our work we are presented with goods that have been rejected, bankrupt stock and the like, and we are extremely grateful. The warehouse is never empty. One gentleman rang us up asking if we had found some boots with pound notes folded in the toe. We had not, so some person received those boots and we hope they found the money.

One lady rang up nearly in tears. Her friend had been on a once-in-a-lifetime holiday to China and had lent her the holiday video to see. Inadvertently it had come out of her car at the warehouse with the things she was delivering, please could we find it? Many, many things had come in since she had been at the warehouse but about a week later we came across it – she was so relieved!

Many lovely things happen, too, which are such a blessing to us all.

There was the time I was at the warehouse on my own. It was bitterly cold and after an hour or so I developed a sore throat and reached into my anorak pocket for the Polo mints that I always keep there. However, there were none in the pocket and I realized that I had changed anoraks. So I thought, "Well, I will just have to go out and buy some," only to realize that I had not brought my purse with me either and so did not have any money. I remember saying to the Lord that I had been foolish and my throat was now getting worse, so would He please just touch me and make it better so that I could carry on.

I then lifted the next black bag of clothes up onto the table and emptied out the contents as usual. It was a bag of men's clothes and out of a trouser pocket fell - a packet of Polo mints. I could not believe it; we very rarely get things left in pockets. This was the first time it had happened and there were the Polo mints.

I picked them up, sat on the table and cried, wondering at the Lord's love and tenderness. I felt He was saying, "You are not here on your own, I am here as well and this is a little gift from Me to you."

Then I began to think further, remembering that that batch of clothing had come in months ago. So, months previously, the Lord knew that I was going to pray that prayer and He had arranged for them to be left in the pocket. Then again I remembered that the ladies had been in earlier in the week. How was it they had not picked up that bag? Then, how was it I chose to pick up that particular bag from the pile after I had prayed? In the end I had to say like the psalmist, "Lord, Your ways are too wonderful for me to understand." But, Lord, how grateful I am that I, and others who belong to You, can experience Your love and tenderness as You watch over us day by day.

"...for He is always thinking about you and watching everything that concerns you." 1 Peter 5:7. *The Living Bible*

A number of British young men who go on aid trips to Romania end up by marrying Romanian girls. They certainly get a bargain. The young girls are taught from a very young age to be homemakers, and by the time they are ten years old most of them can not only cook but also wash, iron and sew as well. The cooking is not just plain cooking. They are also taught how to make bread, doughnuts, and other such things.

One young man met a young Romanian lady, fell in love and they were going to be married in Romania. The wedding cake was made here. We had a telephone call asking if we could take the wedding cake to Romania for him. Of course we could, and so it went very carefully on the lorry. It was extremely well packed and delivered safely. We arrived in the tiny village en route to our destination late one night and were given a bag full of hot home-made doughnuts as a thank you.

Spectacles go to the churches and often in the services the people go forward taking their Bibles, testing the glasses to see which pair is suitable for them. One lady, after receiving her glasses asked to be allowed to read the scriptures the following Sunday as a thanksgiving to the Lord. Things for which we no longer have a need are such a blessing to other brothers and sisters.

A lady who works with the deaf in Cardiff has contact with a pastor who is working with the deaf in Oradea. She prepares many parcels for his work and we are more than happy to take them out.

The many broken watches and clocks that come into the warehouse have meant so much to a Christian brother in Romania. He is a brilliant watchmaker and he mends everything that we take him, being then able to sell them to provide money for his family. His wife said that when the boxes come he is like a child at Christmas impatient to open them and see what is inside.

We have taken many things to a pastor in Iasi who crossed over the border of Romania into Moldova. He was an evangelist to the Jewish people and took our aid in with him. God has done a wonderful work among the Jewish people and many came to know the Lord Jesus as the Messiah.

It has been wonderful to see the photographs of them being baptized, sometimes whole families. We praise the Lord for this brother and were encouraged when he said to us, "You know, the quality of the things that you bring is so excellent, it is a joy for me to distribute them, and a real testimony for the Lord to those receiving them." He also receives the *Vineyard*, which is a Christian booklet for Jewish people. Another contact we have made in Cluj also distributes this literature.

We not only take unusual things over but we often *do* unusual things while we are there, apart from our normal work.

A pastor in Cluj needed to build an extension on the top of his house to accommodate his family and the many visitors whom he puts up. The extension was being built in wood and the saw mill where the wood was coming from was two hundred miles away. A Christian brother owned the mill, but somehow the wood had to be transported from there. We juggled our schedule and arrived at the mill early in the morning. We worked for many, many hours in a chain filling the three trucks with the timber that was needed. It was absolutely exhausting work because some of the timber was very heavy. We placed a cassette player within hearing distance and put on praise tapes to keep us going. We had to keep using the more lively tapes because the slower ones slowed us down! At the end of the day, hardly able to stand up, we had the joy of sharing a meal with the owner and his family; we all sang and praised the Lord together. We then drove the trucks to Cluj, where, of course, the wood had to be unloaded!

CHAPTER 12

Jehovah Jireh ~ God Provides

I had finished all the packing one day when I found a half bag of clothes on the back of a shelf. I did not want to leave them there but wanted to pack them to get them out of the way. They were really nice ladies clothes (a small size) and I remembered that I had packed a box for a pastor's wife who was a small size and, although I had not filled the box as full as I would have liked, I had sealed it rather than leave it open. I found the box, re-opened it and carefully folded the clothes on top, but there were two items I just could not get in no matter how hard I tried. So I re-sealed the box thinking that I would just have to leave the dress, which was very expensive-looking, and the sweater, which was very dressy and obviously also very expensive, on the shelf.

Then I spotted a box on the shelf that I had not been able to quite fill. It was a box of watches and clocks for the Christian watchmaker. I thought that if I put the coat and the blouse in the top of that box I would be able to seal it and send it rather than leave it for next time. The family would be able to pass on the clothes. They fitted in exactly and I was able to re-seal the box and put it in the stack for delivery.

When we arrived in Romania we carried the boxes up to the watchmaker's apartment. We had arrived late on the Saturday night so after having a meal we had gone straight to bed.

The next day was Easter Sunday and we were waiting for the two oldest girls of the family to join us so that we could go to church. Loredanna was seventeen years old and Jetta fourteen; they were lovely Christian girls, and we were very fond of them. The door was flung open and there they stood, Loredanna in the dress and Jetta with the sweater on over a black skirt. They looked absolutely stunning and the clothes fitted them perfectly.

"What do you think Mrs. Ann? Don't they look good? They are the exact fit. Thank you so much for sending them - the Lord has answered our prayer."

They then told us the story.

They had been chosen to sing in the church choir on Easter Sunday and so much wanted something nice to wear. They knew that their family could not afford to buy anything for them, so unbeknown to their mother and father, they had prayed each night to the Lord that somehow He would send them something special to wear. On the Saturday they had said to each other, "Well, maybe the Lord does not feel that it is an important thing in our lives. We must be satisfied with what we have," - which was very little.

When we had gone to bed on the Saturday night, their father could not resist opening one of the boxes to look at the collection of clocks and watches. He happened to open the box with the two items of clothing in and that is when the girls knew that the Lord had indeed answered their prayer. I think that they were the most expensively-dressed young people in the choir that morning!

Thank You again, Lord, for guiding me even though I did not know it.

We had decided to take a holiday in Cornwall for a couple of weeks and as the weather was particularly bad one week we called in at a local hall where an auction was going to be held the next day. We thought it would be interesting to see what items were for sale. As we wandered around Alan came across some tins of nails and began to show an interest in them, saying that if they could be bought cheaply, he wouldn't mind buying them. I could not believe it; our garage is full of all sorts of bits and pieces, including nails, which have been there for years.

"What on earth do you want more nails for?" I asked. I was about to add, *you're no good at DIY anyway*, but thought better of it!

"Well, they could come in useful."

"For what? To sit in the garage with the others?"

"Well, I want to buy them," he said stubbornly. "I'm going to ask if I can put a reserve price on them." I gave in - I knew he was determined. He came back, "I've put a reserve price on them for a couple of pounds, and I have to ring tomorrow to see if my bid was accepted." I sighed and thought, well, he probably won't get them at that low price anyway.

As I wandered near the back of the hall, I spotted an adult tricycle. I was intrigued; it isn't very often you see one of these and it was in excellent condition. I called Alan over to look at it. "If that could be bought cheaply I wouldn't mind buying it," I said. He looked at me in amazement.

"What, for goodness sake, would you do with *that*? You grumbled about my nails, this is even worse."

"Hmm, but if it *was* sold cheaply it would be a good thing to have."

"Have for what? I can't see you cycling around on it."

"No, not me. I don't know really, it's just so nice."

"Ann, the very least you could put on it as a reserve price would be fifty pounds. You probably wouldn't get it for that, but just suppose you did, what are you going to do with it then?"

I felt a bit disgruntled, but could see his point. "Oh, well, never mind," I said, "It was just an idea."

The next day Alan telephoned to see if his bid for the nails had been accepted. Disaster! It had, and so we traipsed back to the hall to pick them up, with me moaning all the way about the waste of time, waste of money and more rubbish in the garage. I could see that Alan was beginning to feel his purchase was a bit silly now too, so thought that I had better be quiet. Men's pride and that sort of thing!

We paid for them and took them to the car. "I suppose it was a bit silly to buy them," muttered Alan sheepishly.

"No, no, I'm sure they'll come in useful." I said, feeling rather false.

Our next trip was now coming up. Everything was ready, but Alan decided to ring a brother in Romania to check if there were any last-minute things that perhaps the church needed. Their old church was much too small and they were in the process of building a new one. We had on the lorry many things to help them.

"Is there anything that you are desperate for before we leave?" Alan asked.

"Yes, there is one thing which is really urgent. I don't suppose you can get us some special nails could you? They are for fixing the roof and, of course, we can't get them here."

"What size and kind?" Alan asked. Our friend told him. The ones that Alan had bought were the exact

124

kind and size, and also the quantity that was needed. I felt particularly chastened as I realized how I had tried to put him off buying them - but his turn was to come.

We set off to Romania (nails on board!) and again went around the country with many things. On our journey we had to go to a village to deliver a particular parcel. As we were about to leave the lady asked if we would mind waiting a few minutes as there was someone who would like to see us and he had something to ask us. We said, "Yes, of course," and waited for him to arrive.

The door opened a little later and in came someone struggling to walk because he was handicapped. He explained that as a child his father had beaten him and thrown him down the stairs and as a result he could not walk properly. The doctor had assured him, although he did not know how, that if he could somehow get an adult tricycle that would be all he would need to strengthen his legs. "Would there be any possibility," he asked, "of bringing me out one of these?" We could hardly believe what we were hearing.

We talked about it afterwards. We never cease to be amazed at the way the Lord works. Nails and a tricycle - two completely insignificant and unrelated items which had occasioned a little pique and yet God had known how both were needed.

"Perhaps you'll listen more carefully to me in future," I said.

"Are you saying that whenever you want to buy something I had better agree?"

We collapsed in laughter, but then apologized to the Lord that we did not get it right, asking Him to undertake for the tricycle.

A month later we were able to get a tricycle from Social Services.

Just before one of the journeys, there was a knock on our door one evening and a man stood there. He said that he had heard about our work. He was a bathroom stockist and was selling up. Would we like to have ten brand new assorted coloured toilet seats? It was really kind of him and to be honest, we did not like to refuse. We took them in, thanked him and shut the door, then looked at each other. What were we going to do with ten toilet seats? However, we were now learning and often things had been given us which we had not asked for, but we had put them on the lorry and the Lord had had somebody special in mind for them. So on to the lorry went the toilet seats.

On this particular journey, we had to visit a lot of homes in succession. When we get to homes, we always take the opportunity of going to the toilet because we never know when we will find the next one.

I used the toilet in the first house and saw that it had no toilet seat. Off the lorry came one of the toilet seats. Alan went to the toilet in the next house - no seat. Off came another one.

We visited ten houses in succession without any toilet seats and, of course, in Romania the bathrooms and toilets are not like ours – they do not have the luxury of colour schemes - so we just gave each house the nearest one to hand.

When we got to house number ten we just *knew* they were not going to have a toilet seat either - and they didn't. However, they were a little bit better off than the other families and they had painted their walls brown. As we lifted the last toilet seat from the lorry we looked at each other. It was brown! The Lord knew all about the toilet seats and added an extra special touch to co-ordinate the colour of the last one. He is so amazing.

Again, here is another story showing how God often guides without our realizing it and how He really is a God of each individual circumstance.

In the early years of travelling, before setting off for Romania, Alan used to go to the local Cash & Carry to get some basic goods which we took over to the pastors and their wives. It was always the same; pasta, rice, tea, coffee, dried milk, that sort of thing. However, on one particular occasion he returned with an extra item, a large, catering size block of cheese.

I was really surprised because this is not one of the items that we take and I asked him who the cheese was for.

"Nobody, really. I just saw it there and thought that I would get it."

"Well, what are we going to do with it?"

"I don't know, but perhaps if we took it to one of the pastors he could cut it up and share it out. It would be a real treat for people especially some of the elderly folk."

"Well, yes," I conceded, "it would."

So when the trucks were loaded, on went the cheese. We travelled around Romania visiting many pastors with things they needed for their churches. When we got to the pastor's house in Cluj and started to unload the things for him, I suddenly spotted the cheese. Actually, I hadn't noticed it before and had forgotten all about it. I said to Alan, "The cheese is still here, Alan. What are we going to do about it?"

"I'll tell you what, take it in to the pastor with his other things," he said. "He can share it out as I suggested before."

I went into the house with a box of food and the huge piece of cheese resting on top. The pastor's wife was in the kitchen together with their son who was about nine years old at the time. When I appeared in the doorway, she took one look at me and started to cry, whilst the son started jumping up and down saying, "I told you, I told you that Jesus would answer my prayer."

"What's the matter?" I asked, seeing her tears. She told me that about a week previously her young son had sat at the breakfast table and said, "Mum, I'm fed up with bread and margarine. Why can't we have some cheese?" He loved cheese.

She had replied, "Now you know there is no cheese in the shops at the moment and even if there was, I couldn't afford to buy it."

"Well," said her son, "I am going to pray to Jesus that He will send us some cheese." Every morning he would come to the breakfast table saying, "I've asked Jesus to send me some cheese again today." She admitted that her tears were because of her lack of faith, because each morning as her son told her this she would think, "Oh, no! He is going to be so disappointed."

What a wonderful God we have! Alan did not feel "led" or "guided" to pick up the cheese but the Lord was guiding him even though he did not know it because He knew that a little boy in Romania was trusting Him for cheese.

CHAPTER 13

Four Christian Women

Let me introduce you to four special ladies, from whom I learned a lot and who greatly humbled me.

We had gone to deliver a parcel to a family and we had some difficulty in finding the place but eventually arrived at this little house. We knocked on the door and a lady answered. At a guess I would say she was in her late fifties. We had our Romanian friend with us to interpret. We explained that we were delivering a parcel from her adoptive family in Wales and conveyed their greetings. She was so full of joy to see us and began to praise the Lord. Our friend explained to us that we had arrived with her parcel at just the right time. She had been a widow for sixteen years. She had eight children and was living in this tiny three-roomed house.

She and the children had no shoes on their feet, the house had a flagstone floor and she was obviously very poor, yet she was so happy and joyful. I felt tears begin to well up inside me. I sat down on the bed and just cried, thinking to myself, "It's alright. She won't realize why I'm crying." She came gently over to me, putting her arm around my shoulder and knelt beside me. She spoke to me with such tenderness through the interpreter.

"What does she say?" I asked.

"She says, 'Don't cry for me because I am poor; I know that I am poor, but my riches are in heaven'."

I cried all the more. I felt so small, so humbled.

Lord, I'm so sorry I am looking at what she hasn't got yet You are reminding me through this dear sister that she has the most important thing – her treasure is in heaven.

Again, on one of our journeys we needed to deliver a parcel to a place where we had not been before. We had been held up and arrived late in the evening. This lady lived in an apartment and, like the other sister, was desperately poor. A blanket was hitched across the window acting as a curtain. We did not have our friend with us this time to interpret, but managed to get her to understand why we had come, placing the box on the floor.

We asked if we could possibly stay the night as it was too late to reach our planned destination, and she nodded her head, obviously delighted to have us. She indicated for us to sit down and started putting mugs and plates on the table. The Romanian people always want to give you something to eat no matter what the time is, and she was no exception. We protested, "No, no, please, we are fine," but she just smiled and carried on.

She spoke to one of the children who immediately left the room and came back within seconds with half a pot of jam, which she placed on the table. Then she carried in half a loaf of bread and proceeded to slice it up, after which we were called to the table. We sat down, said grace, and helped ourselves to the bread and jam. The bread was mouldy and we realized that the jam had been obtained from a neighbour, but her delight and love in serving us made me want to weep again.

When I thought of the fuss we so often make if we are having guests and preparing a meal for them, I recognized that we in our country have so much to learn about true hospitality. As we ate she stood in front of us and, her face aglow, sang hymns to us. I noticed the men were choking a little also; it was very moving. However, this was not all. I was to be humbled again. As we got up from the table she sat me down and brought me a bowl of water and towel in order to wash my feet.

Lord, as far as hospitality is concerned, I realize I have not even begun. Please bless this sister who has so very little yet gave all that she had, even her very self.

I remember another family we visited. We did not normally take their parcel to them but that particular day we had a little spare time and so suggested to our friends who normally deliver for us that it would be nice to visit one of the families. We said that we did not mind which one, so they chose a family who lived not far away. We arrived at the end of a village where there was an old railway outbuilding divided into five rooms. In each room lived a family, and in that room they lived, ate and slept. The family we visited had five children and the father was out of work.

As I gazed around this small room all I could see for sleeping arrangements was a double bed, which was broken. I whispered to our friend, "Where do they all sleep?" She whispered back, "Like sardines, all in that one bed."

"Well, where do they wash and go to the toilet?" I whispered again. She beckoned me to go outside and as Alan and the men were talking to the husband and wife, they didn't notice us as we slipped away.

Running the length of the building was a

corrugated iron covering and under this was one shower – a rusty pipe and a hole in a cement floor - which apparently rarely had hot water. Next to this is what I can only describe as a horse trough where they did their washing (cold water) and further on, two holes in the ground – no doors, just a bit of a screen - which was the toilet, all shared by the five families. The smell, as you can imagine, was terrible. I just thought of all that I had at home and felt quite upset. Imagine washing my clothes in cold water; imagine using a toilet like this, especially perhaps at night without lighting.

We went back inside and before we left I asked this Christian lady if there was something special I could tell her adoptive family in Wales that she needed. She took both my hands in hers, and with a beautiful smile said, "No, thank you, I have everything that I need." She must have seen my bewildered look, because she repeated, "I have everything that I need, because I have Jesus." I turned away so that she would not see the tears in my eyes, I felt so humbled.

Lord, You have shown me so much through this dear sister, I feel broken inside. I not only feel that I am not grateful enough for all that You have given me, but I also ask myself, would I have answered in that way or would I have asked for one of the many things that she so obviously needed?

It reminded me how once before I had been given six really pretty boxes of soap and had taken them to a poor lady with whom we stay. It would be a real luxury for her, I thought. She was delighted with the soaps and kept looking at them and smelling them. Her face lit up as she said, "I know five ladies who would love to have one of these soaps. I can give them one each and have one for myself."

I remember thinking at the time, "Lord, would I have done that or would I have put them away thinking I've got enough to last me for quite a while?" The Lord certainly challenges us, doesn't He?

It was bitterly cold, far below freezing, snow on the ground and we were delivering a parcel to a place in the back of beyond. As we pulled up at the house, Alan and the co-driver got out of the lorry and went to the back of it to get the parcel. As I and the interpreter also got out of the lorry I was aware of a very elderly lady standing on something behind the fence of the next house and peering over the top. She called to me in Romanian, "Are you the person the Lord has sent with my food?" I thought quickly. We did have some spare food that we could give her, so I said, "We do have some food that you can have."

She then asked, "Has the Lord sent my shoes with you as well?" She went on to explain that the day before she had prayed to the Lord because she had no food or shoes and told the Lord that she was going to stand in the front garden and wait for the answer to her prayer. She was standing in the snow in bare feet because she had no shoes, waiting for the answer to her prayer. For the first time I had a spare pair of shoes for myself. My boots were a bit broken and I thought that if they went completely I would be in difficulty. The shoes were on the back of the lorry. I had not needed them as yet and they were brand new.

All the other shoes had been delivered, so I said to her, "Yes, I do have a pair of shoes that you can have."

I went to the back of the lorry and collected some food and the shoes and took them to her. "I do hope they fit you," I said as I handed over the shoes.

"Oh, they will fit me," she said. "God knows my exact size," and she put them on. They fitted her perfectly. She said, "Multumesc," (which is "thank you" in Romanian) raised her hands to heaven and was obviously praising the Lord, and then went into her little house and shut the door. She did not say, "Who is this lady speaking a strange language and why has this big lorry parked up outside my house?" The Lord had answered her prayer and that was the most important thing.

We called that lady "the shoe lady" and visited her many times afterwards with things especially for her. Are we missing out on so much because in many ways we are so materially well off we do not have to trust God for everyday things?

I remember saying to Alan, "What great faith that dear lady had!" And I remember Alan's reply – "Yes, Ann, she did have great faith, but she had great faith in a great God!"

We heard a lovely story about a family who received a parcel. They are supported by a group of ladies in Newport. We had left their parcel to be delivered by one of our other helpers. He had taken the parcel, but nobody was there so he had left it with a neighbour. A few days later he had a letter from the person who received it. He and his three children were out visiting his wife in hospital. He was on his way home with tears in his eyes because the children were hungry and he had nothing to give them when he got to his house. The neighbour handed him his parcel – it had been delivered just in time. How overjoyed the ladies in Newport were to hear that!

CHAPTER 14

Items From Romania

In Oradea, there is a large Christian publishing outlet called *Romflair*. A Christian who owned a publishing firm in the U.K. felt called to the ministry and donated the printing presses and all that was needed. Christians are employed there and they are very, very busy. We often bring literature back to this country for them. Many people have found it cheaper to have it printed there. Of course this means that it takes us a little longer getting home because we have to have papers for this to go through customs, but we are glad to be able to do it. It was lovely to go there one day and see thousands of *Every Day with Jesus* printed in the Romanian language.

Over the years we have sold thousands of drinking mugs and plates, and have used the profit for baby milk where it is needed. We collect them from a factory in Cluj. Many people take them to sell for us and usually come back for more. We know of one man who actually sold them at a funeral - well, after the funeral actually, when people were having something to eat!

There is a Christian lady who makes beautiful ceramics in her garage. They are hand-made and hand-painted and so lovely that they too sell very quickly, providing her an income also.

The people of Romania are very creative and many ladies give us linen cutwork, and lace-work to bring back and sell for them. We sell a lot of linen cloths made by a lady in the east of Romania. There are a group of Christians in the village but they have no church. The money we have taken back so far has laid the foundations of the church and any further money will be used to build the church itself.

We have also sold a lot of oil paintings for a Christian man whose work is superb. They have proved very popular and he is able to provide for his family with the money.

Another man makes beautiful wickerwork, so we often bring back cane settees, armchairs, magazine racks and coffee tables. They are so nicely made and so strong, we never have any problem selling them and of course, they are so much cheaper than you would pay in the shops. He then uses the money for his family.

CHAPTER 15

"To Be Content"

As I get older I do, I freely admit, forget some things, but with the Romanian work I am pretty good and do not usually make mistakes. That is why I was completely baffled when we arrived at a house with a double bed which I had thought they needed, but they did not.

When we go to the different places in Romania, I always write down what is needed so that if possible we can bring it the next time. For the family that we were now with, I had written in my notebook "a double bed." So after taking in the parcels from the family in Cardiff who had adopted them, we said, "Right, now we will bring in the bed." They looked at us mystified, "But we have no need of a double bed," said the lady and she proceeded to show me the bedrooms, which confirmed what she had said; they certainly did not need another bed. "I'm so sorry," I said to Alan, "I have honestly no idea how I made that mistake. It's actually written down in my notebook." Alan grumbled about taking space on the lorry for something that was not needed. I took his point because the bed had taken up space which was precious.

"Well, we will just have to find a home for it," he said. It was to be sooner than he thought.

The next town that we visited was Deva. We were calling on the young couple called Carmen and Darius. We left many things there for them to deliver. They took things to an orphanage and to a pastor in the village who was poor and had many poor people in his congregation. We also left many parcels for poor families who had been adopted by families in Cardiff. We put all the things in their little house and then I said to Carmen, "Carmen, would there be one of the families that you know of who would need a double bed? We have a spare one on the lorry."

She looked at me. "Is it truly spare? I mean, are you sure it is not needed elsewhere?"

I assured her that it was truly spare. "Do you think," she enquired tentatively, "that Darius and I could have it? Would you mind, would that be alright?"

"Of course, Carmen, but I had no idea that you needed a bed." I said. She took me by the hand into the bedroom. They had two young boys. In the bedroom were a cot and two bunk beds. She explained that the baby slept in the cot; she slept on the top bunk, the other little boy on the bottom one and her husband on the floor.

They had been married five years and had never asked us for a bed. "There are so many needs that are greater than ours," she explained. We took in the bed she cried and hugged me tight. "I cannot believe that Darius and I are going to be sleeping in the same bed. Oh! It is wonderful." We took in blankets and sheets, pillows and a duvet. Every time I go there she again takes me by the hand and pointing to the bed and then pointing upwards she says, "My gift from God."

Did I make a mistake? I'm not too sure that I did. I believe that God could see the need and because they were concerned solely about the needs of others and did not ask for themselves, He provided them with a love gift.

I told Alan this. "You're always right, aren't you," he laughed.

"Not always, just most of the time," I answered teasingly.

On one of our stops at the home of a couple called Matiu and Victoria he told us the story of the lock.

There was a family who regularly attended church and always sat together. Over a period of months he noticed that there was always a different member of the family missing at each service. Eventually he enquired of the father why and was told that one member of the family had to stay home each week as the lock had broken on the door of their house and they could not afford to buy a new one. Matiu remembered that in a box I had packed for him to distribute there was a lock which he still had at home. He went home, took the lock to the man's house and it fitted perfectly.

I did not even remember putting the lock in the box; obviously there had been a space and I had looked around for something to fill it – which was the lock. I did not know the need of this brother for a lock, but the Lord did, and again He had guided me without my knowing it.

Another time I had packed some music books for the choirmaster in Oradea Church (he is an American who was called to Romania to take charge of the music). One of the congregation had spoken to him a few weeks before and asked him when he next returned for a break to America if he could get him a suit carrier, as the one he had got him many years before was now broken. Ken said that he would but that he was not actually going to America for quite a while.

When he opened our box, on top of the books was a suit carrier. He could not believe it. He was amazed, but not as amazed as the man who received it.

Again, the box obviously needed something firm on top and that was what I found.

Lord, You are so amazing and so very, very wonderful.

On another occasion a radio was pushed into one of Matiu's boxes to fill a space. He decided to take it to his mother who lived on the top of a mountain, hoping that she could pick up the all-day Christian programme that is broadcast from Oradea. What a joy it was for her! She put batteries in it and took it with her as she tended the animals. However, the most wonderful thing was that when it was sermon time, she gathered all the ladies in the village and they come now regularly to listen to the sermon. Who knows what the Lord will bring to pass through this?

I mentioned before how hard I would find it to live in Romania. However, I was talking to a man who had had no choice but to go and live there.

He had been a pilot in Saddam Hussein's air force. He was a high-ranking official with a large house, swimming pool and servants. He and his family lived in the lap of luxury. Then he and his family were wonderfully saved. It became known that he was a Christian and he knew that he would have to flee the country. The only country that would accept him was Romania. He was well-educated and highly intelligent. He told me his story outside the church in Oradea. Our friend Matiu had shown us where he was now living, a very poor ground-floor apartment in a block of dirty flats.

"I left, you know, with only one suitcase - everything else my family and I had to leave behind," he told me.

My eyes filled with tears as I imagined myself in that situation, closing my front door, leaving my house and possessions, never to return.

"I'm so sorry. What a situation to be in! That must have been so awful for you. Apart from leaving your country you have had to leave your home as well."

"Yes, but I've got something much better," he said. "What is that compared with what I have now?"

I looked at him not quite understanding what he was saying.

He smiled gently as he took my hands, "I have Jesus, and all that was left behind is nothing compared with knowing Him."

My eyes filled up again and I felt so small.

Lord, although I always hope as a Christian that I'm not materialistic, You have shown me today that perhaps that's not quite true.

Again, Lord, I say that I love You but those can be easy words. Would I be prepared at 84 years of age to walk four miles to church and four miles home again in all winds and weathers, and not only on Sundays but in the week to the prayer meeting as well?

That is what Matiu's mother does, and does with joy. She loves the Lord so much but she puts her words into action.

Lord, You are so challenging.

We constantly meet people who make great sacrifices for the Lord.

Mary Lou was quite a wealthy American widow who could have had an easy life, yet the Lord called her to Romania. She set up a library for the students in the Bible College in Oradea. She was in Romania for six years. She personally poured a lot of her money into the project and set up a magnificent library that was to be one of the best in Eastern Europe. Her sons told her that she was spending their inheritance and refused to let her see the grandchildren when she returned home for short respites. How her heart ached, how many times she wept as we talked together! She had had to sacrifice not only the love of her children but her grandchildren as well by being obedient to the Lord.

She suffered for many years, but the Lord honoured her commitment and now today she is back home in America and her sons and grandchildren are in loving contact with her again.

Following the Lord is not always easy.

CHAPTER 16

Families

It has been a joy to deliver some of the family parcels we take and to visit brothers and sisters in their own homes. There are so many stories to tell about the families. Come and visit a few of them with me.

One family lives in a town called Tirgoviste. They are a lovely Christian couple and have sixteen children. Many Christian families have large families, because they have been taught in error that God is pleased with them if they do. Because of the lack of trained pastors in some places this is a difficulty. However, this is not the case with all large families. In Ceausescu's time contraception was banned and the people were encouraged to have large families. There is contraception available now in some areas, but it would be far too expensive for most people to buy.

This lovely family is always such a joy to visit. The father is a pastor in the local church and each child sings and plays an instrument. So, of course, when we go there they play and sing for us, and the youngest one stands up and recites poetry. There is no shyness here - they do not have to be persuaded to sing and play for us; they delight in doing so. The children range from four years to nineteen years. Like all Romanians, they always insist that we have something to eat and they are thrilled to see their brothers and sisters from the West.

As we pass the kitchen on the way in and out, I love to glance inside simply to see the old-fashioned clothes airer hanging from the ceiling. It is usually full of socks and underwear and I always wonder to myself, how the mother manages to cope with all these children.

Their youngest boy called Bogden was the one who used to recite poetry to us, as well as sing. On one of our visits we were told that he had leukaemia and was seriously ill. Even though he now looked so frail, he continued to sing and recite to us. Almost inevitably, on a later visit we were told amidst tears that Bogden had died a few months previously. One of his older sisters told us this story.

She said that Bogden knew that he was soon going to be with Jesus and one day he came to her and said, "Maria, will you teach me a new song so that when I arrive in heaven and see Jesus I can sing it to Him?" So she taught him a new song which he practised until he was word perfect. I guess Jesus was delighted to hear him sing that song as He welcomed him into heaven!

Once we were given some money from a family in Cardiff for their family. We took it with the boxes that they had also sent. When we got there the mother opened the door. She had been crying and when we went into the room, we saw the rest of the family sitting around the table, obviously upset and the father with the Bible opened in front of him. They explained why they were so tearful. The youngest son needed an urgent operation but it had to be paid for. In fact there is a National Health Service in Romania, but because of the corruption and because doctors feel they are badly paid, you always have to pay. This poor family did not have the money and knew that without this operation their son would die.

We handed over the money that had been given to us by the Cardiff family. They opened it amidst many tears. It was the exact amount that was needed for the operation. Can you imagine how the Cardiff family felt to know that God had spoken to them and even instructed them as to the right amount?

We regularly visit a family out in the country, taking a parcel from their adoptive family in Newport. What a joy it is to visit them! There was an elderly husband and his wife, plus the wife's sister. They grew their own vegetables, and had a pig and some chickens. The house was always so cold and they worked so hard to survive.

He had actually been in Gherla prison with Pastor Richard Wurmbrand and had suffered much. He was very frail but obviously loved the Lord so much. Whenever we went there he played the piano for us while his wife sang from a handwritten hymnbook. It always moved us deeply. To come away, she always gave us a bottle of homemade fruit juice and a cake.

The sister lived in a building like a shed in the garden and when we went to visit them one day we wondered why she did not come to greet us with her sister and brother-in-law. They took us to her and lying on a bed was the sister paralysed down the one side obviously having had some sort of stroke – she looked so ill. We speak very little Romanian and they spoke no English, but they indicated to us clearly that they wanted us to lay hands on her and pray. They were very persistent and we felt a bit uncomfortable because we realized that they were hoping for complete healing, explaining in their limited way that the two of them could not manage the work without her.

I whispered to Alan, "What a responsibility they have given us; neither of us as far as we know has been given the gift of healing. But then, it's the Lord who heals, isn't it? It's just that they're sort of relying on us and I feel so inadequate."

"But then," said Alan, "The Lord is more than adequate; we can't refuse, can we?"

We smiled at the couple and indicated that, of course, we would pray for the sister. We both laid hands on her together and prayed not only in English but also in tongues and then stood back. She remained motionless on the bed, but the couple seemed satisfied, so after giving them hugs and kisses we beat a hasty retreat.

Healing is so difficult to understand. One has to face the fact that the Lord does not always heal, although He is more than able. Being totally honest, I said to Alan, "I'm scared to go back in a few months time, in case she is in the same position as she is now." They seemed to be relying on us.

A few months later we returned to the little house and as we got out of the lorry and approached the gate, the sister came running to meet us. The Lord had wonderfully healed her. How we praised His wonderful name!

Thank You Lord that You are more than adequate to meet every need.

We were involved in another situation regarding healing which did not have such a happy ending. We had met a young couple whose little boy had a serious heart problem. Apparently he should have been operated on at birth, but they did not do that sort of operation in Romania

Laurentio was by now four years old and a very sick little boy. The parents had been told that an operation could be done in the U.K. with a fifty-fifty chance of success. We promised that we would make enquiries with a doctor friend on returning to Cardiff. The doctor flew over to see Laurentio and assess the situation, and decided that he would like to help this young couple. So Laurentio was brought to Cardiff for the operation with his father who spoke English. His mother and younger brother would join them at a later stage.

The family was well loved by people in Cardiff who knew them from visits to Romania, and how we prayed that God would heal this dear little boy! He had the operation, which was successful, but unfortunately during the recovery period he suffered brain damage, and was left unable to speak or move – he was virtually paralysed.

What a terrible blow it was to all of us who had regularly visited the hospital, prayed and looked after the parents for so many months, and how heartbreaking for this couple who had so hoped for a miracle! They had to return to Romania with a child who was brain-damaged and paralysed. We cried with them, finding it so hard to understand. God could have healed but he chose not to. Why, oh why, was the unspoken question on all our lips.

It was so difficult for the couple when they returned home. The wife could no longer work because Laurentio needed full-time care. They also felt cut off from their church for a while. It was not really anyone's fault. We think it was just that the brothers and sisters in the church felt so awful at what had happened. They did not know what to say or do and yet they both needed so badly the support of the church which they did eventually get.

On our later visits it was always upsetting to see little Laurentio lying motionless on the bed settee. Through the generosity of friends in Cardiff his mother was able to employ a physiotherapist to come in a couple of days a week to help him. As she attended Laurentio and spoke with the parents they shared with her their deep Christian faith. She was moved as she heard about Jesus, and gave her heart to the Lord, as did her daughter who is now studying in the Bible College in Oradea.

Later Laurentio was to pass away – gone to be with Jesus. His little life, although he did not know it, had been used to save two lost souls.

CHAPTER 17

Lydia, Mihaela and Mirella

Lydia, who lives high in the mountains in Com Rucar, is a sweet young girl. Sometimes when we call with the family's parcels her parents are out in the mountains taking care of the sheep and goats. Since she was about eleven years old she has looked after us, laying the table, cooking pork and potatoes, struggling to speak in her little bit of English.

Before we leave she gets her Bible out and looks through it before writing a verse with the reference on a slip of paper for us to read as we travel on. These verses always touch my heart. No television, video or any of the other things which others of her age would enjoy here. Such a solitary lonely life for a little girl, yet even at that age her face shone with the love of Jesus as she waited on us.

We were finally given two large round goats' cheeses that her parents had made. It was at this house we were once given a huge stuffed seagull as a present. The man explained in his limited English that he had found it on the side of the road and had brought it home and stuffed it for us. "It smelled a bit," he said, because he did not have the proper material with which to stuff it. It *did* smell, and looked horrible, the wings were stretched out fully and the eyes looked scary. The only way we could carry it on the lorry was by tying it up and suspending it from the side. What a terrible sight!

"Where are you going to put it?" Alan asked me.

"In the lounge?"

"Thank you, Alan, I know that it was given with love, but I think that it will be jettisoned long before it reaches Cardiff!"

One of our dubious claims to fame is that we visited the Siret orphanage made famous by Anneka Rice, even before she did.

We had been told how dreadful it was and had been asked to go and see the place with a view to helping in some way. Words just cannot describe our feelings; we were so terribly upset by the situation there. Even the men were moved to tears. We also shed tears of frustration as we realized that this project was far too big for us. The whole drainage system needed to be over-hauled for a start and there were so many major things that also needed doing. We were so thrilled when a matter of months later *Challenge Anneka* took the project on and was able to make such a difference to the lives of the children there. From time to time as we travelled to Romania we would pop into the orphanage to see the progress being made and during these visits struck up a friendship with a young girl called Mihaela.

Mihaela had been put in the orphanage at six years of age. She was not strictly an orphan. Her father had been an alcoholic and her mother had been too poor to look after her. Mihaela, although very intelligent, had spina bifida and her mother just could not cope as she lived in a couple of rooms with no running water. Mihaela was sixteen years of age when we first met her, and we had become very fond of her, taking a parcel whenever we went. She spoke a little English but wanted to learn more so we gave her an English Bible, which she read avidly.

As I wrote before, in Romania when you reach 23 years of age and are still in the orphanage, you are often put into the nearest old people's home. As Mihaela was nearing her 23rd birthday she wept as she pointed to the old people's hospital which was at the back of the orphanage.

"That's where I will have to go when I'm 23." We wept also because we knew the place. We were supporting the hospital with many things and already there were a couple of young people in there. It was such a dismal and depressing place. There were many old men and women in there, many of whom had mental problems as well. We could not bear to think of Mihaela going there. However, we realized that there was nothing that we were going to be able to do. It broke our hearts.

About a month later we were asked to speak at a coffee morning at our church, just filling them in about our last trip. We did not have long to speak, so Alan and I decided on what we felt were the most important things to share. As Alan spoke about the situation he said, "We really don't realize how fortunate we are to live in this country," and he told them Mihaela's story.

As we drank a cup of coffee after speaking, a man came up to us. "I would like to buy that young lady you mentioned an apartment. I believe that the Lord has laid it on my heart." We could hardly believe what we were hearing.

Lord, how wonderful! Can we, with Your help and the help of this brother, really bring this to pass?

Weeks later, Alan and one of our trustees drove to Romania with the money that was needed (by now others had given also). We had Christian contacts in Bucharest who would help us to buy Mihaela an apartment, and Mihaela's mother lived near

Bucharest. The apartment was bought, Alan returned home and about a month later went back with a team to paint and decorate the apartment and furnish it for her. Mihaela's mother was located and reunited with her. Siret is three hundred miles from Bucharest so they rarely saw each other.

Today Mihaela lives happily with her mother in Bucharest. Her mother has a job, which brings in a wage, and Mihaela is cared for by Dranka, one of the other girls who was also in the orphanage and due to go to the old people's home. They had been friends in Siret and we were so pleased to be able to help her also in this way by bringing her to Bucharest. It is so wonderful to see how the Lord moved in this situation. Not only Mihaela, but also her mother and Dranka have been given a real life at last.

At the time of writing Mihaela has not professed to being a Christian, but she reads the Bible and has started going to church. We also talk to her about the Lord. We pray that the Lord who saved her from the fate of the old people's home will save her soul, so that as well as a home here on earth, she will have a home in heaven.

Thank you, dear brother, for being obedient to the Lord's prompting. He has done more than you could have ever thought or imagined.

After settling Mihaela in her apartment we felt that it would be good if we could get her an electric wheelchair. This would enable her to get out and give her some independence. Consequently we put it down on our next needs list but disappointingly nothing materialized. It was a few weeks before we were due to leave for Romania and still nothing. Then one day Alan took a phone call in his office from a lady who offered an electric wheelchair which had belonged to her mother who had recently died. She was living in Wembley and explained how she had heard of the work. She had a married daughter who, with her husband, had been working abroad with the Leprosy Mission. They had had to return to this country because she was ill. They had nowhere to live and so scoured the country for a church that temporarily did not have a minister and where there might be an empty manse. They were told that there was one in Grangetown in Cardiff, so came to see it. The caretaker also showed them over the church and as they passed through the vestibule there was a stack of our literature on the table. The church supports us and two of our trustees are members there. She took some leaflets and back home her mother "happened" to pick up the needs list and saw the need for an electric wheelchair. What intricate steps the Lord had taken to secure the wheelchair for Mihaela! He fitted every piece of the jigsaw into place to complete the whole picture.

Lord, thank You that nothing is too much trouble for You and nothing is too difficult for You to work out.

"Is anything too hard for the Lord...?" Genesis 18:14. *New International Version.*

After Mihaela had her wheelchair we realized that she had difficulty going out because there were steps outside the apartment, and Alan felt if we could get a ramp to go over the steps that would be ideal. He had thought about it for some time and then, on one of the journeys, his co-driver was a mechanical engineer, and so he asked him what he thought. "A ramp should solve the problem," he said, so Alan knew that a wheelchair ramp was indeed feasible.

On that particular return journey, he dropped the co-driver home in Newport at midnight on a Monday and at nine o'clock the next day Alan had an excited phone call from him.

"I'm ringing from Abergavenny," the man said.

"What on earth are you doing there this time in the morning?" Alan asked.

"Well, I had promised my wife before I went away that I would take her to Abergavenny, and so here I am." (I was impressed!) "The point is, I pulled up to park only to see a wheelchair ramp being put up outside the back door of the van next to me. It's just the size of the one we need. I have got all the details, where to get it and I am going there this afternoon."

He purchased the ramp and telephoned us in the evening to say not only had he bought it, but he had been given the money to cover the complete cost.

Mihaela is now able to go out of her apartment in her wheelchair - God's perfect timing yet again.

We are given a lot of wool which we take over for Mihaela. She then crochets large blankets which we bring back and sell in order to help her and her family. Also, another couple who have adopted a girl suffering from spina bifida regularly send us money for Mihaela.

Mirella was doing evangelistic work with her husband in the town of Oradea. She had been ill and received an injection from an unqualified nurse. As a result she was quite badly paralysed in the legs. She so much wanted to continue God's work but could not walk very far because of the paralysis. She wrote saying, "I know that it is probably impossible but if you ever have an electric scooter come into the warehouse, would you consider giving it to me?" Well, of course, we have never had one of those in;

they would be far too expensive to give away and we could not see any likelihood of us ever getting one.

Two weeks later we were offered an electric scooter which was almost brand new. Only Alan, Mirella and I were aware of the need – apart, of course, from one other very important person. God, our loving heavenly Father!

Mirella is now able to be independent and to continue serving the Lord in Oradea.

CHAPTER 18

God Meets The Need

We support two Christian High Schools in Romania, one in Cluj and the other in Oradea. Pastor Beni's wife from a Baptist church in Cluj is called Nora and she is a teacher in the first school. A few years ago she visited the U.K. and was taken to a school fayre. She thought it was a wonderful idea and asked us that if we ever had anything sent to the warehouse that we could not use for the other places we support, could we send them to her as she would like to hold a school fayre? Because the government has little money the school is always badly in need of writing materials and Nora's plan was to use the money made in the school fayre to purchase what was needed. The staff would make cakes and they would try to raise money that way.

We do have many things sent to us that are not suitable for the places that we support and since that request we have sent them to Nora for the school fayre. Everyone enjoys them, apparently, and she is able to buy some of the things the school so badly needs with the money raised. They have even been able to put a new roof on the school and are busy building an extension.

Sometimes people ask us where our money comes from to keep the charity running and to buy the many things that are needed.

"Do you fund-raise?" they ask.

"No, we don't."

Two very happy brides wearing the wedding dresses which we took for them.

The parents of these twins are dead and their grandmother looks after them. We were given clothes for twins and here are the Romanian twins dressed in one of the outfits.

A family receives items from Carmen and Dorin, Ploiesti.

Friends from Lliswerry Baptist Church, Newport, holding a garden party in aid of Support for Romania.

Weymouth Baptist Church organises a stall on the sea front each year in aid of Support for Romania.

At St David's Praise and Christmas Praise held at St David's Hall, Cardiff, we have been allowed to sell items that we bring back from Romania. We so enjoy meeting many of our friends and supporters at these gatherings.

Lorredana and Jetta who prayed for new clothes for Easter Sunday. They stand in the designer clothes that the Lord sent them.

Ann with the dear lady who was waiting in the front garden for the answer to her prayers. She was 83 years of age and standing barefoot in the snow.

Alan and Ann showing how the weather was when the 'Shoe Lady' was waiting in the front garden.

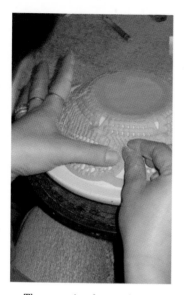

The ceramics that we bring back to sell are hand-made and hand-painted by a christian lady in her garage.

Tabitha with one of her lovely hand-made tablecloths that we bring back to sell. The proceeds are helping to build a church.

Matiu's mother who is in her
eighties walks over the mountain
three miles to church twice on a
Sunday and also during the
week.

Carmen and Darius and their
family from Deva who received
the double bed.

The man and his family from Iraq who, although they left everything
behind in Iraq, say that having Jesus in their life is more important
than possessions.

The musical family in Tirgoviste entertains us. They are supported by a family who live near Pontypridd.

The elderly husband and wife who pleaded with us to pray for her sister. They are supported by a family from Newport.

Ann with the sister whom the Lord healed through prayer and the laying-on of hands. Doesn't she look well!

Mihaela (right), the young lady we were able to take from Siret orphanage and put in an apartment in Bucharest due to the kindness of our supporters. Helped by her mother and her friend and carer Dranka, she holds one of the blankets which they make for us to bring back and sell, which helps with their finances.

Mirella, who became unable to walk due to a faulty injection at the hospital. She can now continue to help her husband with their evangelistic work.

A teacher at the Christian High School in Cluj receives one of the boxes with goods to sell at the school fayre.

The minibus which was purchased for the Orphanage and Old People's home, paid for by the lady from Llandrindod Wells.

The house that the poor family were living in before moving to a better one through the generosity of a christian lady. She had received a legacy and used it to buy 'her family' the new house.

This is the 'new' house.

"Well, how does the money come in?"

"The Lord brings in the money in various ways and through the love and generosity of his people."

The world is continuously fund-raising for this event or another and people are asked to sponsor many things but our Heavenly Father does not always work like that. I guess He has no need to. What does the Lord say?

> "The earth is the Lord's
> and everything in it."
> PSALM 24:1 *New International Version*

This was once brought home to us in a remarkable way.

Alan and I were preparing our next needs list. As we did so we suddenly became aware that for about eighteen months we had said on the list that £6,500 was needed for a minibus. This was to be shared between an orphanage and the old people's home we support. We also realized that nothing had come in towards this need, not even one pound. So we wondered whether perhaps it should come off the list. After all, we always have the four thousand pounds needed for baby milk, and money comes in for various other things. People only have a limited amount of money, maybe we should take it off. We discussed this and then Alan said, "I'll tell you what, we'll put it in once more and if nothing happens this time, we will not ask again." So, on the list it went.

The lists had not been out very long when one day Alan was in his office and he received a telephone call. It was from a lady who had seen our needs list on a church hall notice board. As far as we knew she was not a Christian but ran a young girls' dance troupe which practised in the hall. She told Alan that she had done many shows for charity and would be really happy to do as many shows as was necessary to raise money for the minibus. Her shows were always well supported and she knew without doubt that she could raise a lot, if not all of the money that was needed.

Alan was taken aback; we had not done anything like this before - the Lord had always brought the money in. It was so kind of this lady to offer, so he thanked her very much and said that he would talk it over with me.

As we talked about it, it just did not sit right. We appreciated so much her kindness, but for a start everything would be coming under the name of *Support For Romania*. What would they be doing? If it was a young girls' dance troupe what sort of dances would they be doing? Some can be very suggestive, as can the clothing that they might wear. What sort of songs would they sing? If there was a compère, what jokes would he tell? What if they had a raffle? We would not have been happy with any of that and it would have been in the charity's name. So we decided that we would have to thank the lady and decline her very kind offer – which was not going to be easy. Well, it was for Alan because he gave *me* the job of writing to her!

However, before I could do this Alan had another phone call. It was another lady and she said, "I'm ringing up about the minibus. I would like to buy it."

Again, Alan was nonplussed. "You mean that you would like to give something towards it." he suggested.

"No, no, I want to buy it," rejoined the lady. To which Alan replied, "You do realize that the cost is £6,500 don't you?"

"Yes that's right," said the lady. "I just needed to

know who to make the cheque out to? I'm actually ringing from Llandrindod Wells."

"But how, then, did you know about this?" asked Alan. "We have nobody on our mailing list in Llandrindod Wells."

This was the lady's story. She had telephoned her niece who lived in Neath who told her she had been busy that day packing sweets for the children of Romania. She had felt that she too would like to pack some sweets for the children and had asked her niece what she should get and how she should wrap them. The niece decided that instead of reading the list over the telephone, she would send it to her aunt. So she did and the aunt saw the need for money for the minibus.

"I'm a Christian," she said, "and the Lord laid this need on my heart. That's why I want to send you the cheque."

We were able to buy the minibus and deliver it on a later journey to the orphanage and old people's home.

Alan and I discussed this remarkable situation later and felt that the Lord was saying, "You did right. I have always brought in everything that you need. I own the cattle on a thousand hills and when the need and the time are right I will bring the money in." Alan said that it reminded him of a verse in Scripture that says,

Don't let the world around you squeeze you into its own mould. Romans 12:2 *J.B. Phillips*

Thank You Lord, for a lesson learned and for making it much easier to write to the first lady and thank her for her kind offer telling her that God had already brought the money in.

Every year we go on holiday to the same place in Portugal. (Our sons think we are really boring). Whilst we are there we always worship at the English-speaking International Evangelical Church. The people there know that we are involved in a work in Romania and asked us if we would be prepared to go over in the winter to speak at a coffee morning which they held once a month. They said that we could stay in the church flat so that we would only have to pay our airfare. We agreed, especially as we had air miles which we could use for the flight. So in February we went over and we had a good time sharing about the work and also afterwards having a chat to people over a coffee. There were two couples who were on holiday from Norwich. They talked with us, and then asked if we would be prepared to go to Norwich in September to speak at their church about our work. We said that we would be delighted. We were on holiday and relaxed and didn't really think how far Norwich was from Cardiff.

When September came we were "up to our eyes" in work and extremely busy, as we were going to Romania the next month. We truly wished we had not made the commitment and said to ourselves that we had made a mistake in saying that we would go. Nevertheless, we went, as promised, and how glad we were that we did as we were so blessed, not only as we shared with the fellowship about our work, but also as we heard how the Lord was working amongst them and how many had become Christians in the last year. We were so touched when they said that they wanted to support us prayerfully, practically and financially, and furthermore that they wanted to adopt a Romanian family. They were prepared to come all the way from

Norwich to Cardiff to deliver the goods and dutifully hired a van and drove down to Cardiff. However, the blessing did not end there!

Not long after our visit, we received a letter from a lady who had been in the service at which we had spoken. She explained that she actually lived in New Zealand but had come to Norwich for a few weeks to organize the moving of her older brother into a home as he needed care. She was a Christian and as we had been speaking, she had felt moved to send us a gift. She asked particularly that it be used for the supply of baby milk. As I held the cheque and marvelled at people's love and generosity, I said to Alan, "How far are we with our finances for baby milk? How much more money do we need?"

"I don't know," he replied, "I haven't checked it yet. I haven't really had time."

"Well, could you check it when you have a minute," I responded. "I would like to see how much more we need to reach the required amount."

A few hours later Alan came down from the office. "About the money for the baby milk," he said, "we are still short of a good amount."

"How much?" I asked.

"A lot, Ann, £1700 pounds."

I went to the drawer and took out the lady's cheque. I gave it to Alan watching his face as he unfolded it. It was for £1700!

He turns our weaknesses into His opportunities, so that the glory goes to Him!

I have already mentioned that we support Christian social workers who deal with various families with many needs, and that we also have many families in South Wales and further afield, who adopt and support poor families in Romania.

One day we received a letter from the social workers asking would there be any possibility of us finding thirteen more sponsors as they had found thirteen more desperately poor families who were badly in need of help.

We actually had people at this end who were waiting for a family, including a lady from the Welsh valleys. She was a relatively young Christian but desperately wanted to support a family. So I told her about the request and sent on the details that I had.

She was so keen! She wanted to know their birthdays, so that she could send them cards. She wanted to know the clothes and shoe sizes, and so much wanted to do all that she could to get things right for her family. So I contacted the social workers to get the required information.

I had a reply with the information, but also the social workers went into more detail about how extremely poor they were, that there were five people in the family, mother and father and three children, that the house was made of wood and only had two rooms which had earth floors. It had no running water or electricity and was practically falling down. The letter went on to say that, of course, really they desperately needed another house and that there was one in the village for sale but that it cost two thousand pounds, which naturally they had no hope or possibility of buying.

I realized that they were just sharing with us about the house for sale and I did not want to send the whole letter containing this information to the lady concerned in case she thought that the social workers were asking for money, which I knew they weren't. So I decided to send my own letter, leaving out about the house that was for sale. I told Alan what I was going to do and a few days later went to the office to collect the original letter so that I could take out just the information about the birthdays and the sizes.

I was looking for it when Alan came in and asked me what I was looking for. When I told him he said, "Oh, I have actually done that for you to save you a job." I was pleased and then asked, "You did remove the information about the house which was for sale, didn't you?" Here I have to say that he said I did not tell him that I was going to take the information off (but I did, I did! Sorry, Alan!) And so the lady received the letter with the information on it that I did not want her to have. I felt terrible and was upset with Alan who continued to protest that I had not told him.

What on earth would she think? I asked myself. I was soon to know.

Another sister from the same church had been instrumental in telling this lady about adopting a family. Two days later my friend came on the phone to me asking if we could meet up for coffee. She needed to talk to me about the letter that had been sent to the lady. I readily agreed, feeling so bad about it all and wanting to explain that the information given about the house that was for sale was only meant for me. It was not intended to go any further.

So I met my friend as arranged. As we settled down with our coffees she said, "Ann, it's about the two thousand pounds for the house."

"I know," I said, "I guessed it was," and I wanted to explain that this information was not meant to go to the lady concerned. She stopped me, "Ann, go no further. I want to tell you that the lady wants to buy the house."

"What! How can she possibly do that? I know that

she is by no means well off, she couldn't afford two thousand pounds."

"Ann, two days before she received your letter, she had been told that she had been left two thousand pounds in a will and she wants to buy the house with that money." I could hardly believe what I was hearing. I asked her, "What about her family, what about the things they need?"

My friend looked straight at me, "Ann, they are behind her every step of the way. They've said they want her to do it because they have more than enough."

Seeing my uncertainty she said, "I know; I wasn't sure about it until she said to me, 'Don't worry, I might be a young Christian but I'm not stupid. I know when the Lord speaks to me and He has.'"

So Alan was able to take out the sum needed for the social workers to buy the house for this poor family.

God must have prompted Alan to send that letter because He knew about the two thousand pounds. He also knew how much this lady loved Him and was prepared to be obedient to His voice.

Alan's smug comment was, "You see, that shows you didn't tell me not to send the information about the house."

To which my indignant reply was, "That doesn't prove a thing, except that the Lord used your forgetfulness."

Does it really matter? God completed His plan despite us both, as He always does.

CHAPTER 19

Blackboards and an OHP

One day we had a telephone call from our youngest son, Timothy, asking if we would do him a favour. He and his wife ran a coffee house in Birmingham and we tried to visit as often as we could. We were going to see them the following week and he asked if we could pick up some china for the coffee house on the way. We agreed, but were a little startled to be informed that the china needed to be picked up in Stoke-on-Trent, which is certainly not on the way to Birmingham; far from it. Nevertheless, we said we would go. We had a dreadful journey as it was a Friday. There had been a serious accident on the M6, the traffic was heavy and we took ages to get to Stoke-on-Trent. We were exhausted when we finally arrived.

We followed Timothy's directions, found the china warehouse, picked up the things he needed and made for Birmingham. We had intended staying the night (which we did) and taking the china to the coffee house in the morning. He went on to work and told us to take the car into the basement of the building where his coffee house was and take the china up in the lift.

This we did, had a coffee with him (which I think we paid for) and returned to the basement to get the car. As we made our way to the car we saw a skip and on it was an overhead projector. Alan said, "It looks as though they are throwing that out. Maybe just a bulb has gone, or there is something minor that is wrong with it. If so we could have it for Romania."

So Alan went back upstairs to ask Timothy who was the official we should see about it. He told him to find Security and have a word with them which Alan did, and one of the security men came back with Alan to the basement.

While Alan was gone, I had spotted four large blackboards which were about the size of a door surrounded by lovely wooden frames. So when Alan came back, I pointed those out to him as well. The security man took one look and said, "Well, if you don't have them they'll only be going to the rubbish tip — so help yourselves." Apparently they were refurbishing some offices on the third floor.

So into the hatchback went the overhead projector and the blackboards. We were thrilled.

[Actually, this was far less complicated than one visit we made to our local rubbish tip. There we saw a large quantity of Dexion shelving in one of the skips. It was a deep skip and Alan had to lower me into it for me to pass the shelving out to him. We were thrilled. It was brand new and just what a Romanian doctor had requested for his clinic. I passed the last piece out to Alan and waited for him to come and pull me out. Then I heard the engine of the van start up. I managed to peer over the top of the skip to see Alan about to pull away. I shouted, "Alan, Alan what about me? I'm still in the skip." A look of horror came over his face. "Darling, I'm so sorry. I was so delighted with the shelving, I completely forgot about you." Say no more!]

But back to the overhead projector and blackboards. We unloaded them at the warehouse the following Monday morning. The first thing Alan did was plug in the projector to see what was wrong with it. It was absolutely perfect, nothing wrong with it whatsoever – what a wasteful society we are, but what a wonderful bonus for us. We were delighted. In the afternoon our helper Mac came to the warehouse. He had been with us on our journey one month previously.

I should explain here that when experienced people were with us we often used to send them with a lorry to a particular place while we went elsewhere. On the previous trip we had sent Mac to a pastor in a place called Jimbolia, telling him to ask the pastor for a list of the things he needed so that if possible, we could get them for him on our next journey. (The lists are now received by email.)

Back at the warehouse on that Monday afternoon Mac reached into his pocket. "I'm sorry this is a little late coming to you. To tell you the truth, I'd completely forgotten about it but these are the items that Adrian the pastor would like, if it's at all possible." He handed Alan the list and Alan opened it up. It read......

Dear Alan,
If it is at all possible there are two things that I would very much need for the church - an overhead projector and some blackboards.

Mac had received this a month previously!

We gazed at each other in amazement. These were the two things that we had just picked up. Why had our son asked us to go to Stoke-on Trent on that particular day? How was it that we "happened" to go to that basement at that particular time? We were shown yet again that with God things don't just happen, they are planned.

"Before they call I will answer." Isaiah 65:24. *New International Version.*

Thank You, Lord, for allowing us to see that verse of Scripture come true right before our eyes.

CHAPTER 20

CHAPTER 20

It's His Work

A little while ago I heard a story about a young girl who was at a missionary meeting in her church listening to an elderly man speaking. Because she was young, she was bored and not interested. But then her ears pricked up as she heard the man say, "Now, I would like to tell you how I proposed to my wife," and she thought, "Now, this will be interesting." Her face fell, however, when he said, "I proposed to my wife by quoting her verse 3 of Psalm 34, and she accepted." The young girl did not understand; in her eyes that did not seem much of a proposal. But it was, in fact, a very special proposal for that verse says, in the *New International Version*

> Glorify the Lord with me:
> Let us exalt his name together.

Alan and I have been married for 48 years but I like to think that seventeen years ago, when we started this work, Alan could have made a similar proposal to me about our venture using those very same words. For that is the desire of our hearts, not only to show the Lord's love and compassion, but to exalt Him as we travel back and forth to Romania. We thank Him for the joy and the privilege of working alongside Him in His work.

We are frequently asked, "When do you think this work will come to an end?" Our answer is always the same, "God called us to the work, and when He calls you to do something for Him, you keep on doing it until He tells you to stop, and He has not told us to stop yet."

We have found that to *know* God's will is life's greatest treasure, and to *do* God's will is life's greatest pleasure, and together we have learned so much of Him in the process.